C000213040

Louise Dearman

British musical-theatre actress Louise Dearman is widely known for her many performances both on national tours and in London's West End.

Following her graduation from Laine Theatre Arts, where she won the Musical Theatre and Opera Award, she joined the touring cast of *Joseph and the Amazing Technicolor Dreamcoat* in the role of the Narrator. She then went on to play Jan in the UK tour of *Grease* in 2000, before returning in 2003 to London's Victoria Palace Theatre to play the same role. Further past highlights include Sarah Brown for the national tour of *Guys and Dolls*, and Mimi in the Piccadilly Theatre production of the show; Lucy Harris in the UK tour of *Jekyll and Hyde*; Debbie in the 2007 Edinburgh Festival production of *Debbie Does Dallas*; Grizabella in the international production of *Cats*; Eva Peron in the UK touring production of *Evita*; and becoming the first actress to star as both Galinda and Elphaba in the hit musical *Wicked*. Louise also created the role of Mrs D in the world premiere of *Water Babies*.

Louise has headlined at London's St James Theatre, starred in *An Evening of Movies and Musicals* at the Apollo Victoria Theatre and at Swansea's Grand Theatre, featured on *Friday Night is Music Night* on BBC Radio 2, and played Lois Lane/Bianca in *Kiss Me, Kate* staged as part of the BBC Proms.

Louise Dearman's first album *You and I* was released in 2005, and was followed by *Here Comes the Sun* (2012), and *It's Time* (2013).

www.louisedearman.com
@LouiseDearman

Mark Evans

Mark Evans is a Welsh-born actor, singer, dancer and West End star, currently living and working in New York City. He has played Elder Price in the North American tour of *The Book of Mormon*; Sam Wheat in *Ghost: The Musical*, Fiyero in *Wicked* and Troy Bolton in *High School Musical* in London; and Brad in *The Rocky Horror Show,* Curly in *Oklahoma!* and Caleb in *Seven Brides for Seven Brothers* on tour of the UK.

Mark was a finalist in the BBC One competition *Eurovision: Your Country Needs You*, to find a singer for the UK's 2009 Eurovision entry composed by Andrew Lloyd Webber. He has since worked frequently in television and radio, particularly as a presenter on the Welsh-language channel S4C. He hosted his own TV special *Noson Yng Nghwmni Mark Evans*, and in 2011 he created the title role of the eccentric composer in *Marcaroni*, one of the most popular children's TV shows ever made for S4C. His film credits include the Syfy Channel's *Lake Placid 3* and short film *Dead Hungry*.

Mark is an accomplished and experienced teacher and is passionate about theatre education. In 2006, he created West End in Wales, an annual musical-theatre summer school in North Wales, for young talent to be trained and coached by Mark and other West End professionals.

In 2011, Mark released his debut solo album, *The Journey Home*, which features both English- and Welsh-language songs. Due to popular demand, a deluxe edition, with all the songs sung in English, was released in 2012.

www.markevansonline.co.uk
@MarkHEvans

Louise DEARMAN Mark EVANS

SECRETS OF STAGE SUCCESS

Your Questions Answered

NICK HERN BOOKS
London
www.nickhernbooks.co.uk

A NICK HERN BOOK

Secrets of Stage Success
first published in Great Britain in 2015
by Nick Hern Books Limited, The Glasshouse,
49a Goldhawk Road, London W12 8QP

Copyright © 2015 Louise Dearman and Mark Evans

Louise Dearman and Mark Evans have asserted their moral right to be identified as the authors of this work

Cover image and illustrations copyright © 2015
Mark Manley (www.markmanley.co.uk)

Designed and typeset by Nick Hern Books
Printed and bound in Great Britain by
Ashford Colour Press, Gosport, Hampshire

A CIP catalogue record for this book is available from the British Library

ISBN 978 1 84842 375 6

For our Mama
Rebecca Sichel-Coates
Thanks for all your constant guidance,
love and support

Contents

Introduction

We were working together in the West End production of the mega-musical *Wicked*, Mark as Fiyero, and Louise at the time as Galinda (though she went on to play Elphaba too). Whenever we weren't dancing through life or defying gravity, we would chat about our similar backgrounds and interests: how we both had a passion for performing from a very young age; how we worked hard at our hobbies through our teenage years; our experiences training at the same college, although not at the same time; what it was like starting to audition for – and get – roles and moving through a succession of professional productions; and our shared opinions and experiences – the good and the bad – that come along with any career in the entertainment industry.

We are both asked for advice from aspiring performers, sometimes at stage door after a performance, from letters sent to theatres or via our agents, and increasingly on social media. There is such demand for information about how to break in to the entertainment industry from young people who, exactly like us when we were younger, want to make it their career. So we decided that we could combine our experiences and knowledge in writing a handbook about how today's commercial-theatre industry works, and to offer some words of advice to anyone who'd like to make it their livelihood too.

In order to make the book as helpful as possible, and to answer the questions that people really want and need the answers to, we decided to invite you to tell us what you wanted to know. We encouraged anyone, of any age, anywhere in the world, to post questions via a special website that we set up. To the many, many hundreds of you who did, THANK YOU! Your questions were interesting, thought-provoking, intelligent and revealing; and we've answered as many as we thought we could cover in one book. We really appreciate everything you asked, and we genuinely couldn't have written this book without you (if we've answered your question, then your name's in the back of the book). Even if you're not planning on a career on stage yourself, but have an active interest in theatre, we hope that the book draws back the curtain and shines a spotlight onto the realities of life as a performer.

The book is divided into four chapters that cover, broadly, training for a career in theatre; auditioning for roles; getting jobs and performing; and then managing and maintaining a lifelong career. Most of the questions we've answered together, but if one of us has a specific experience or an anecdote that's relevant, we've included that too, indicated by a little 'headshot'. We've also written about our most memorable moments in the business which are dotted between the chapters on shaded grey pages.

Of course, everything that follows comes from our own experiences, performing in some of the biggest West End musicals of the last decade – so it's naturally focused on musical theatre, and mainly on opportunities in the UK. We've also made a conscious decision only to cover working on stage, rather than what it's like being a performer on screen. Other performers will have had different experiences and may have different advice. But what's here is an honest reflection of our ideas and opinions, that come from spending thousands of hours in classes, workshops, audition rooms, rehearsal spaces and, of course, on stage.

In some ways, we are writing this book for earlier incarnations of ourselves. It contains all the secrets of this crazy, wonderful, exhausting, exciting, bewildering but brilliant profession, that we wished we'd known when we were starting out. If you're in that position now, dreaming of a career on the stage, we hope that this book reveals the secrets you need to know.

We hope you enjoy reading it.

Louise and Mark x

Part One

SECRETS OF LEARNING YOUR CRAFT

Training and Developing

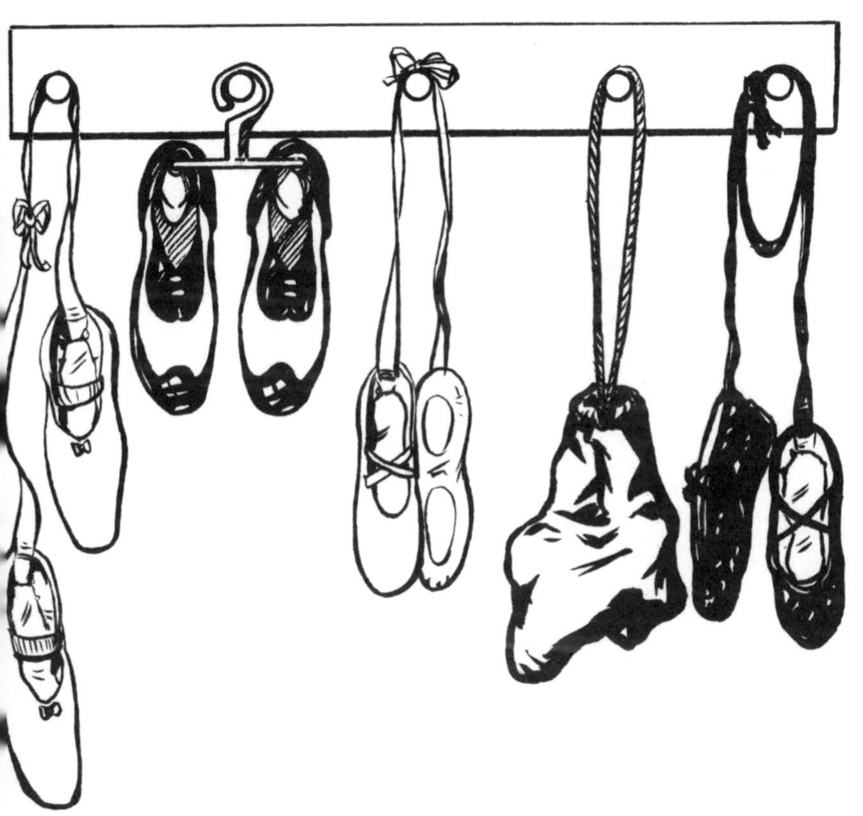

Do you think anyone can train themselves to be an actor or is it mainly natural ability and talent?

If you define an actor as someone who 'interprets and portrays a dramatic character', then it could be argued that anyone can do it. When we were children, we would make believe all the time, using our imaginations effortlessly to portray cops and robbers, astronauts in space, explorers in the jungle, or pretend to be our favourite pop stars. Later in life, if we've ever read a bedtime story to a child, then we can all put on the voice of the Big Bad Wolf, huffing and puffing to blow down the poor little pigs' houses. We also adopt different roles in life all the time, depending on where we are: at work, with our families, down the pub with our friends…

So everyone has a natural ability to make believe and pretend, put on voices and impersonate. And there are certainly those who have a natural gift and talent for connecting to a character on a deep emotional level, and investing in that completely until they almost *become* that other person. But that's not quite the same as being a professional performer, when you need to be able to do it in such a way that connects with a larger audience, and with a certain range of skills and abilities – many of which aren't as natural or intuitive as pretending to be someone else, but all of which can certainly be trained, developed, practised and improved.

For that reason, you should only aim to become a performer if you genuinely have natural abilities. And then we strongly believe that you should train those abilities. Acting is an exposing and vulnerable state to put yourself in, and so learning and developing in a supportive environment is invaluable. You are not a professional performer until you get paid to do it, so you need to keep working hard and developing your craft until someone is confident enough to invest in you by giving you a pay cheque!

How do I choose whether I want to work on stage or backstage?

Ask yourself: do you love performing – and don't want to do anything else? Do you love it enough to commit your time and energy to training hard? Do you have what it takes to enjoy the highs, and to survive the lows? If you don't answer 'Yes' to all these questions, but you love being around the theatre and are interested in what happens behind the curtain, then maybe a job backstage might be for you.

There are the important roles on the creative team – director, musical director, choreographer, designers (of set, costume, lights, sound, and so on). Often these jobs require a specialist training, though are sometimes done by people who have been performers themselves. Choreographers are often former dancers. Similarly, there's an established route from people working up through the ensemble to being resident and assistant directors, responsible for looking after the show on a daily basis, up to directing productions themselves. Most of these roles, though, are done towards the start of productions, during the preparation, rehearsals and getting the show up and running; they're not responsible for being present every day, working on the production from night to night.

There are lots of technical and backstage staff who are in the theatre every day, working just as often, and just as hard, as the performers on stage. To work backstage, it helps to have a calm, quiet and quick mind, and to be able to deal with situations efficiently without panic! The options here include stage management and stage crew, lighting and sound operators and technicians, carpenters, construction (including mechanical parts), flymen (who operate moving scenery), and the wigs, make-up and costume departments.

If you want to work in one of these roles, the best route would be to study for a qualification in Performing Arts – such as a BTEC (Business and Technology Education Council) – which will offer you a practical approach to learning without missing any of the crucial theory on the subject. You might find useful on-the-job training opportunities at a theatre – amateur or professional – near to where you live, and you should certainly get as much as experience as you can. There are some very specific kinds of work backstage, such as carpentry, and for these you might want to focus on Science and Design Technology at school, as these subjects will be the most useful to you. Another option, later on, is to take a degree in stage management or technical theatre, which are offered by many of the major drama schools.

If you want to work in theatre, then don't forget that there are always opportunities to work front-of-house or in box offices. Many performers rely on income from these jobs while they are training, and it can also teach them how different performers deal with different audiences and challenges on stage night after night.

Should I get involved in drama at school or outside of school?

Both drama at school and extra-curricular opportunities out of school have huge benefits – whether you eventually want to work on stage, backstage, or nowhere near a stage at all. We both took part in school drama classes *and* after-school dance, singing and drama lessons. During school, these programmes are a great way to bond with fellow students, and a positive way to build self-confidence, express yourself in a safe environment, and enjoy some relief from academic subjects.

You will probably find that after-school/extra-curricular lessons or groups are where you will really learn and develop your dancing, singing and acting abilities. It's more intensive and focused, especially if you work towards taking exams in your chosen discipline. Getting involved in youth theatre or amateur drama groups can also be an excellent way of getting experience, developing your skills, and spending time with like-minded people. If you join Saturday-morning classes at a stage school (like Stagecoach or Razzamataz) then you will learn a lot of skills, be pushed further, and often the teachers have worked within the entertainment industry themselves and have a good understanding of how it works. Ask around your local area whether anyone can recommend a theatre group, or search online for local opportunities. Your drama teacher at school may be able to offer some advice or there may be fellow pupils who will have similar interests in performing and will be able to recommend somewhere. Either way, any experience in performing will be great for developing your talent, whether it is in or out of school.

Did you do any professional acting work when you were children?

The first time I was properly paid to perform was when I was eighteen, as a dancer in *Aladdin*, a pantomime in Milton Keynes with Claire Sweeney playing the title role. It felt great to be earning a wage for doing what I loved. It was about £400 a week which made me feel rich – it didn't last long though.

When I was twelve, I was in the choir for *Joseph and the Amazing Technicolor Dreamcoat* at the London Palladium. I can't remember what I was paid, but the experience I had working on that show will stay with me for ever. (Don't tell anyone but I'd have done it for free!)

Should I join a talent agency while I'm a child/teenager, or wait until I've finished my education?

There's not really a right or wrong answer to this. We both feel strongly that childhood is a time to be happy and carefree, and there should be no mad rush to jump into working professionally. For us, dancing and singing were hobbies when we were kids – we enjoyed classes, made friends, had fun. Our parents ensured there was balance between our performing and our lives beyond that.

Of course, there *are* children working professionally, very happily, so if you think that you want to join an agency, start auditioning and working – and, above all, that it's your decision and it will make you happy – then of course you can do it, if you have your family's support. But remember that whilst life is short, your childhood is even shorter, and precious. Don't worry about not starting professional work early in life. We started a bit later on, and it hasn't harmed what we wanted to do, or the opportunities we've had.

Should I go to a theatre school, study performing arts at university, or go to drama school?

There are different options for training available to young people in the UK. Drama schools tend to offer a degree-level training for students aged eighteen and above; theatre colleges often offer options for younger students, combining training in performing arts alongside other compulsory academic subjects. Then there are universities that offer performing arts or drama degrees, with a mixture of academic and practical training.

Personally, we both believe that the best avenue to go down if you want to become a performer is a specialist course in a theatre college or drama school, which concentrates on the practical skills and will really teach you what a life in the business will require and demand of you. We don't necessarily think you have to go at the age of sixteen (or earlier), and there is nothing wrong with studying something else at a university or on a foundation course before going on to train professionally in theatre. Many people we know in the business got a degree in a completely different subject before they started their theatre training and it hasn't restricted them in any way.

My 'training' started at the tender age of three. It was, of course, just a hobby back then. I loved dressing up in a tutu and feeling like a little princess in my ballet classes. But it wasn't until the age of twelve that I realised I wanted performing to be more than just a hobby. I'd started going to watch musicals in the West End with my parents and on school trips, and was completely in awe of the performers up there on stage, who were like pop stars to me.

I joined a choir at school and we auditioned for *Joseph and the Amazing Technicolor Dreamcoat* at the London Palladium. We were selected to be 'The Joseph Choir' and went on to perform in the show for several months, alongside

Phillip Schofield in the title role. It was an incredible, eye-opening experience for me and a turning point: from that moment on, there was nothing else I wanted to do in life but perform. I continued with my dance, singing and drama lessons at the Sarah Goffe Theatre School in Leighton Buzzard, and took all my dance exams before auditioning for Laine Theatre Arts, just outside of London, at the age of fifteen. It was a college I desperately wanted to go to, having spent two years taking part in summer schools there – knowing that my idol Ruthie Henshall had trained there. I got in, and at sixteen I headed off on my adventure for the next three years. I will always be grateful for the training and discipline I received at Laine. It taught me that working in the entertainment industry means that you never have time to put your foot on the brake, you will constantly have to work hard, be prepared to learn and develop new skills in every new job, and that it's equally as important to respect those working with and around you to gain their respect back. No one likes a diva!

I left home aged sixteen to train in dance at Preston College Dance Centre in Lancashire. After a year I moved to Laine Theatre Arts to train in musical theatre for three years. For me, having that year before moving to London was so beneficial. It allowed me to get used to living independently, without being too far from my parents. I gradually got used to the best way to approach my training, adapted to dancing all day, every day, and learned how to look after myself accordingly.

When I moved to London I was more advanced than many other boys in my year because I'd already had twelve months' full-time tuition and it was no big deal for me to be away from home. It meant I could embrace my training immediately, unlike some of the sixteen-year-olds around me who found it all so hard to adapt to life without their families. I had the perfect stepping stone between North Wales and London, and certainly don't feel I missed out by doing an extra year.

I've heard drama schools have rejected people for not having enough 'life experience'. Should I have a gap year or get a job before applying for drama school? And what about after?

Taking a gap year – and getting a job, or travelling, or being with your family, or just being lazy – before or after training depends entirely on who you are as an individual and what is happening in your life. A gap year *before* you start training can be a good idea; some time out from education and maybe an opportunity to gain life experiences and earn some money before starting to train.

As for a gap year *afterwards*, we strongly believe that the moment when you complete your professional training is probably the most crucial part of your career. When you graduate, you should realistically be at the very peak of your technique, having spent all your time mastering your craft – so you must choose that moment to try and make your first impression on the industry and set yourself up for as much success as possible.

Think of it this way: there are more than thirty-five drama schools in London alone; each of them have an average of about fifty students graduating every year; so, at the time you graduate, you are merely one of 1,750 new people who are completely unknown in the industry, who all need to get noticed and try to get work. It's really tough at the best of times to have an impact on this business as an unknown, but if you take a gap year *after* graduating, you've then doubled the number of people new to the industry to 3,500. Every year the same number of students get churned out, and there clearly aren't enough jobs for all of them! We would definitely suggest using the time after you graduate to let people know who you are, let them get excited about you, and give yourself a chance to take the industry by storm. At this stage it's less about 'life experience' than it is about getting 'industry experience', and you need to get credits on your CV to move onwards and upwards.

There will be times to take a break later on in your career, if you wish. There have certainly been times when we have felt we just needed a break. Jumping from one job to another is amazing – to be getting a steady income, to be playing some great roles and building up your list of credits – it can then be hard to say, 'No, I won't take that amazing opportunity, because I want some time out.' You have to be confident to turn work down – but sometimes it's necessary.

When I finished touring North America in *The Book of Mormon*, I moved to live permanently in New York City. For the first time I felt it was the perfect opportunity to take a few months out from work, to step back and think about what it was I really wanted to do in order to keep feeling inspired, challenged and passionate. During that time I was able to enjoy seeing my friends, have a social life, and all the freedom that comes with not having to perform a lead role eight times a week. It gave me an incredible outlook on life, a great perspective on my career, and it did me the world of good. So my advice would be that if you want to gain some life experience after school and before training then do it. But don't imagine it will be the one and only opportunity in your career to take a break.

I decided that as soon as left school at sixteen, I wanted to go straight into theatre training. I was itching to get going. At that age, I had many friends who went on to take A levels, some who went straight into job-hunting, and others who just wanted time out from academic studies. We are all unique, and have different needs and ideas of what we want to achieve and when. We only get one life, one chance, so it's important we use it wisely and experience what the world has to offer. If that means a gap year before training is right for you, then it's right.

How do I choose the right training course for me?

Deciding which school, college or university to train at and which course to take is an extremely big decision to make – and a very difficult one, especially if you're as young as sixteen years old. It's basically saying, 'At this stage, right now, I need to decide which avenue I go down for the rest of my life.' Most people are faced with this choice when deciding what to do next in their education, but few other industries demand quite the same amount of focus or financial outlay. Your training might cost in the region of £45,000, so you need to make sure you make sensible, informed choices.

Having said that, you should not be afraid of making these choices. Things aren't the same as they used to be when you would have to telephone a college to request a prospectus to be sent in the mail before deciding if you were going to apply for that school. It's much easier to access information now because of the internet, and you should research all the options available to you. Naturally, every school will point out their positive aspects and never say anything bad about themselves. But the reality is that not all schools are great – and they definitely all have strengths in certain areas more than others.

So here's what we suggest to help you make the decision of where to apply:

Make a list of what you would ideally like to achieve in your life and career in the long run, and if you can be specific, that's better. It can include anything: 'I want to act in a play that has been directed by Nicholas Hytner' or 'I want to perform at Shakespeare's Globe' or 'I want to play Eponine in *Les Misérables*' or 'I want to be a choreographer for cruise-ship shows.'

Once you have a lengthy list, you should be able to work out exactly what sort of career you wish for yourself, and therefore what sort of training you think you will need. That way, when you visit various colleges during your auditions you can use that time to figure out if it is the right place for you by asking the right questions: 'How much Shakespearean technique do you provide?' or 'How many ballet classes will I get?' or 'Will I get regular one-on-one vocal tuition?' You can also make a list of the actors who inspire you and whose work you admire and find out where they trained – look it up online or in a programme biography. If the school trained them to be the performers they've become, then maybe it will work for you too.

It is probably easier at first to work out which colleges are definitely *not* right for you – and then make a list of four or five you are interested in or intrigued by. Find out what their audition requirements are – and what their audition fees are. Most charge a fee to see you at an audition, which can all add up, and is one reason you should only audition at places at which you would really like to be offered a place. Feel free to call them and ask any specific questions you may have.

It's perfectly natural to get very nervous about auditions for drama school – we were certainly both nervous when we auditioned – but you mustn't forget that if you get offered a place at a school, you will be spending three years of your life living there, training there, socialising there, possibly working a part-time job there as well. It's important then to remember that not only are you being assessed by the faculty, but *you* must be making a judgement about whether it's the right place for you to go for your training.

Many theatre colleges offer short summer-school courses where you go and train for a week. It's a wonderful way to explore a particular theatre school and find out if you feel comfortable with those teachers and in that environment. I went to summer schools at Laine Theatre Arts for two years running before deciding that was the college for me. Do your research to find out which summer schools might prove you with useful experience.

Should I make my training specialised (on one or two particular skills) or generalised (on a wider number of different disciplines)?

We think that, at least at the start, you should try and get experience in as many different areas of training as possible. Eventually you will be able to make a clear decision based on which experiences inspired you most; generally it will be the ones you enjoyed the most and made you happiest. For this reason, choosing training opportunities that keep your options open for as long as possible, and give you widest access to a range of disciplines and skills, is invaluable. For musical theatre in particular, you should look for the classic 'triple threat' training, where you will be coached in all aspects of singing, acting and dancing for three years, with the third year probably dominated by preparing and performing in productions and getting ready to enter the industry.

Trust your gut, always do what *you* want to do and don't feel pressured to do anything else. But be realistic as to what you are capable of. We should all aim high and push ourselves to be better in each field, but there are some things that, if we're honest with ourselves, we're just not suited for. You must be able to look at different elements of training, or the demands of a specific role, and know that you simply aren't right for them. That's no excuse to be defeatist though. Your training is the opportunity to have a go at everything on offer. How will you ever know that you're a wonderful acrobat, until you've tried it?

What type of dance is the best or most useful to learn?

Your training should always be geared towards the career you want to have. If you want to be a principal at the Royal Ballet then clearly you need to have trained from a very young age in disciplined ballet technique. Think about who inspires you and do some research on them to see what sort of training they had. As far as the two of us are concerned –

and based on the dancing we've had to do within musical theatre – we would say you need to be trained as much as possible in technique. Ballet and modern are the basic fundamentals, and then you should expect other classes throughout your training in different genres, such as jazz, tap, pas de deux, street, and theatre/Broadway style.

How can I fund my training?

Funding your training can be an overwhelming task that may seem completely impossible to achieve. The average school currently costs at least £12,000 per year for three years, with accommodation and living expenses as additional costs too. It really can be tough, especially as local-authority grants are not as readily available any more.

Firstly, you should certainly check out the website for Drama UK, the national organisation which accredits all the leading drama schools, which will have the most up-to-date advice on funding. There are full details there of the Dance and Drama Awards (DaDAs), which are currently offered at nineteen schools across the UK, and which substantially contribute towards the cost of your training and, in many cases, will help cover maintenance and accommodation costs too.

Many drama schools offer individual scholarships, bursaries and hardship funds which will cover tuition fees and living expenses, so you should enquire with the schools to see what's available, if anything. Some students are sponsored privately by a certain company or individual who will invest in their training because they see potential in them.

If you are not fortunate enough to receive a scholarship or bursary, it is worth reaching out to your local county council for advice and to see if they can recommend anything or offer any funding. Have a meeting with someone at your bank to see what sort of loans they might be able to offer, and investigate government-approved Career Development Loans.

Consider what fundraising you can do on your own behalf. You could organise events or concerts – though do be very clear about where the proceeds of any event will be going, since you are not an official registered charity. Get a part-time job at weekends while you're at school and save your wages. Some people may take a gap year before they train professionally so that they can work every hour and save as much as possible. You may find that you need a part-time job throughout your training to pay your fees, your expenses and keep your head above water.

Funding your training will inevitably be more of a struggle for some people than others, but if you keep yourself focused on all the reasons you are training in the first place, then the stress and effort will be worth it in the end. If you want it enough, then you'll find a way to get there.

What is training at drama school like? Is it stressful?

We both agree that our years of training were some of the best years of our lives: having fun, doing what we loved, being surrounded by people who shared the same passion, and watching and feeling our technique getting better and better week by week.

We wouldn't exactly describe it as stressful but, at times, training can seem like it's an impossible task and you feel that you're not going to improve or get anywhere near your dreams. It is incredibly tough, physically and emotionally, and you have to push yourself to succeed, but also remember to be kind to yourself when it feels like it's getting on top of you.

At Laine Theatre Arts, where we both trained, a typical day starts at 8.45 a.m. when you arrive at college, get changed into your dance wear and warm up for your first class at 9 a.m. The days are divided into classes in dancing, singing and acting right up until 4.40 p.m. This isn't necessarily when your training day will end, because there are always classes after college hours such as audition technique, opera class, extra drama lessons and even assisting teachers with their younger pupils. Then you might have a part-time job in the evenings, or you could be going to the theatre, which is always an important part of training – seeing how other professionals work. Days are very long and you train incredibly hard for three years.

There is a lot of stress put on your body and voice throughout training, so it's important to look after yourself and be sensible. The stressful times really start once you finish your training and have to audition and try to find work. It can be very difficult to accept rejection and move forward, and this can become very upsetting. Give yourself time every day to do something that relaxes you – it can be as simple as reading a book or going to a yoga class. Don't get so absorbed in your training or auditions that you forget about life outside of performing.

If we both look back at the standard of our skills when we started our training at Laine Theatre Arts, and the level we were at after one, two and three years – we were completely different performers. Watching fellow students grow and develop is also an eye-opener. Some people may have started the course as a singer with no dance training, but after intensive lessons and a lot of sweat, they were able to more than hold their own in a dance audition. It's all about how badly you want to achieve your goals and dreams – and how hard you are prepared to work for them.

I am constantly trying to learn new skills and never allow myself to feel satisfied that I am the best I can be, because the reality is: I'm not. We can, of course, be content with who we are – and I certainly am – but I'm an ambitious person and love to learn new things. I'm always learning from every job I do, from every person I work with and even everyday experiences. Whilst on tour round America with *The Book of Mormon*, I took private horse-riding lessons in Atlanta, archery classes in Boston, gun-handling technique in New York, and regularly had dialect coaching to work on various accents – all because I want to keep challenging myself and making myself better and more employable. Just because I've worked for almost ten years doesn't mean I'm going to stop learning new skills. We are forever evolving, which is what enhances us as actors.

How can I improve my vocal range?

Vocal ranges are being challenged more and more, with new musicals often requiring singers to belt consistently at the top notes of their register, then down in the basement of their voices, and then back up top again for a couple of hours every show. It is not only important to have a good range, but also to have a strong voice with the stamina to withstand the vocal responsibilities that come with performing eight shows a week.

The best way to strengthen your voice and increase your range is to find a singing teacher you trust; ideally, one who is very experienced and has a good reputation in the industry. Most good singing teachers can be expensive, especially if you are out of work. Having a weekly lesson for anything from £40–140 can obviously take its toll on your bank balance, but investing in one lesson a month could really make a difference.

An average lesson will be one hour and it's surprising how much you can fit in to that time. All singing teachers will allow you to record the lesson on a Dictaphone or your iPhone, which then means you can repeat the lesson, every day or several times a week, by yourself at home. Making alterations to your vocal range or stamina is not something that can change overnight. It can take weeks, months or, more often than not, years to notice a comfortable difference. So you'll need a lot of practice.

When I toured with *The Book of Mormon*, I had weekly voice lessons for forty-five minutes on Skype with Liz Caplan of Liz Caplan Vocal Studios LLC, who is probably the most sought-after and well-respected voice teacher in New York – if not in America. We only ever did vocal exercises every week. In fact, she hadn't heard me sing a single song until she saw me in the show eleven months after we started our sessions together! I would record those weekly lessons, and label them with what we worked on specifically. For my daily show warm-up I developed a catalogue of voice lessons from which I could select to help me get ready to perform, depending on what I felt needed to happen vocally that day – for instance, if I needed to lower my larynx, clear my nasal cavities or release the tension in my neck. I have worked professionally using my voice successfully for about ten years, but I couldn't have survived *Mormon* without the help of Liz. In my opinion, having a great voice teacher to help you is invaluable.

I have been incredibly fortunate in my career to have played a variety of different roles, all of which required varied vocal styles, ranges and techniques. I have my training to thank for being able to adapt my voice accordingly. If you only sing in one style, you are limiting yourself as to the roles you can play, so it's important to push your vocal boundaries and to develop new techniques regularly.

Even in the one show, Galinda and Elphaba in *Wicked* require completely different singing styles.

During my training at Laine, I had singing lessons every day, in which I worked on musical-theatre and contemporary technique, but I also chose to take opera/classical classes after college hours. At times I was reluctant, it didn't feel like 'my thing', but it taught me so much about finding my soprano voice. On many occasions since, having some classical technique has helped me to protect my voice from overworking my belt and putting too much pressure on my vocal cords.

My most challenging role to date, vocally, was Elphaba. To be able to push the range of my voice to its limits eight times a week was intense to say the least. The day I was offered the role, I got straight on the phone to Mark Meylan, a vocal coach based in London, who has years of experience working with vocalists all over the world. I wanted to make sure I found how to place these huge songs in my voice without putting strain on it and potentially damaging or exhausting it. His vocal exercises helped me to focus and place each sound so it was safe to sing, yet still sounded exciting. I also wanted to keep my tone and not force my voice to sound like another person. I still have his exercises on my iPhone and I practise them religiously to keep my vocal stamina up. Every vocal coach is different and you may have to try a few to find the one you feel most comfortable with.

What kind of training should I do to prevent injuries?

Injuries are, sadly, inevitable. Whilst training and working in such a physically and vocally demanding industry, there will be times when you get sick and injured. You need to ensure you've developed the right techniques to look after yourself, and you must live sensibly and healthily.

You're less likely to get sprains and strains if you look after your body. Commit yourself to working on physical and vocal strength. See a physiotherapist at the first signs of injury; don't wait until it's too late. It's wise to investigate private health insurance as well, which will enable you to access the best medical care and get back onto your feet as quickly as possible. And listen to your body – if it hurts, stop!

How should I approach the final year and the end of my training course, when I'm about to enter the profession?

There is no doubt that, although you work extremely hard and push yourself during your training, it is very comforting to have your friends and teachers around you. You feel safe in your surroundings, you can express yourself, and there is stability and security whilst you are developing as a person and as a performer. Then, as your final year begins, and you start considering life beyond training, it can become very nerve-racking to think that you're suddenly going to be out there doing it alone. Getting into drama school to train as a performer is a great achievement – but it's just the beginning. Just because you've trained, you haven't 'made it'. Yet!

The whole purpose of training is so that, when you graduate, you can start looking for the work you've been preparing for, and developing your career in the industry. Don't be intimidated; be determined. You need to harness a feeling of confidence, self-assurance and focus throughout your training. Here's our checklist for the things you really need to concentrate on when you approach the end of your training course:

- Have a selection of audition songs and monologues prepared that offer a range of styles, genres and characters that you can choose from. (There is more about choosing audition material in Part Two.)

- Be happy and confident with your image. You should be done with trying out new looks and styles and have settled on what you want to look like, remembering that it should be the look that represents your personality best.

- Get professional headshots. You need to have a photoshoot with a professional photographer who will give you a headshot for auditions that represents you as a person and as a performer honestly and effectively. Photo-shoots can be expensive, but it's an investment you have to make because you need to have a good, professional headshot to get good auditions.

- Make sure your CV/résumé is always up to date. Most colleges and teachers will help you with preparing your professional CV. You need one when you're approaching agents, and an agent will create a new one once you sign with them. It's inevitable you probably won't have many or even any credits on there to begin with, but you should never lie. Be honest, state the facts, list the productions you've been involved in during your training, and allow the person reading it to see what your skills are. (There are more tips about headshots and CVs in Part Four.)

- Apply to acting agencies. Many colleges and schools will have some sort of system to support their students in the task of finding professional representation. Some drama schools have their own agency which you're automatically signed to by being a student of theirs. Others will host a showcase where you'll get to perform in front of many agents and industry professionals, who will be there solely to check out the new talent.

  Virtually all schools invite agents to watch some internal classes, shows or final-year productions. If for some reason you do not feel supported in your search for an agent, then you can always take on the task yourself and approach them personally. (There is more advice about agents in Part Two.)

- Be sure you know what you need to do as a newly self-employed professional. The industry is not all teeth, tits and tap shoes – it's about tax too. You need to be ready to earn a wage and take on the responsibilities with your tax payments, and you must register with the Inland Revenue as a self-employed individual. We would advise contacting an accountant even before you graduate so that they can explain to you exactly which receipts you should keep, which invoices and payslips you'll need to file, along with bank statements, and so on. You are a business and you need to be prepared for the somewhat dull tasks that come along with that. (There's more information about managing your finances in Part Four.)

- Make sure you have the appropriate clothing and footwear for auditions: tap shoes, jazz shoes, pointe shoes, knee pads, tights, etc. Obviously, this all depends on what sort of performer you are – if you can't do pointe work then there's no point owning point shoes! When you are called to audition you need to be able to focus on preparing any material, instead of figuring out the basics of what to wear.

- Take photographs. On a more sentimental note, we want to encourage you to take time to cherish the friends and the memories that are made during your training. The years spent at drama school are an incredible period where we form some of the strongest and longest lasting friendships of our lives. The sense of community and safety that you feel whilst training is seldom found again, and so, whilst you need to knuckle down and prepare to take on the world, you should also make sure that you don't miss out on appreciating good times and friendships.

Is it too late to start a career as a performer?

Several of you submitted questions saying you'd started other careers or trained in other disciplines, and weren't sure if it was now too late to consider a career on the stage.

We believe it is never too late in your one short lifetime to realise that what you're currently doing isn't making you happy, and that you want to try and fulfil your dream of performing. So by all means go for it!

We will say this, though: please get opinions of respected teachers of acting, singing or dancing before you make big decisions, because we've all seen those TV talent-show auditions where people genuinely think they are awesome – and they clearly are not. If you know you have the natural talent and ability, and you have been advised to go for it by someone whose opinion is trustworthy, then do it. Voice and dance classes, amateur experience, and a full training are all options that are still open to people looking to enter the profession later in life.

We have friends who retired from performing in their twenties and changed careers, partly because it can be such a gruelling business. Then again, Morgan Freeman was thirty when he first worked on Broadway and was fifty-two by the time of his breakthrough screen role in *Driving Miss Daisy*. The glorious thing about acting is that it's simply a portrayal of life, so there will always be a need for actors of all ages.

I remember exactly how I felt the moment I was about to step foot on stage for the first live show of *Eurovision: Your Country Needs You* back in 2009. This was a reality TV programme on primetime BBC One, in which Andrew Lloyd Webber and the BBC were searching for the UK's entry for the Eurovision Song Contest to be held in Moscow later that year. I had gone through the audition process, and was offered a place in the final six acts that would perform live on television. Eurovision has a bit of a stigma attached to it, and the UK had experienced many years of doing very badly in the contest, so my agent and I had to consider if performing on the programme would be a wise move for me. We decided that no matter what the outcome, getting the national exposure on TV was a great opportunity – providing I did a good job on every live show.

So I really felt the pressure before the first Saturday night broadcast. I still clearly remember it was 10 January 2009, and a lot of my family had come down to the studio in London to support me. The atmosphere backstage was so tense, it would have been so easy to let the pressure get to me. I was standing with the other five acts backstage, and could hear the floor manager counting down: 'Going live in 5, 4, 3, 2… here we go.' Presenter Graham Norton's voice boomed around the studio with a pre-recorded introduction, whilst the monitors, which showed what was being broadcast to the TV audience across the UK, played a montage of the audition process. The voice-over explained how six acts had been selected and how 'Tonight is the night that you at home decide who stays and who will be the first act to go.' Then the show's opening music and titles were played really loud – and my adrenalin was pumping. Here I was, about to be on TV as *myself*, which is so different to what I was used to as an actor playing a character, live in front of seven million viewers. The show cut to Graham in the studio, introducing the acts one by one, and about five seconds before he called my name, I caught a glimpse of my family and friends in the audience, each wearing identical 'Vote for Mark' T-shirts and holding banners plastered with 'Good Luck, Mark!' and photos of my young nieces. In that split second, I was overwhelmed with a feeling of being totally supported, and I filled to the brim with determination. I went out there and had one of the best nights of my life.

My career has been a gentle but steady climb up the ladder of success. I have been in the ensemble, I have been a swing, I've understudied roles, played small roles in large productions, and big roles in small productions – but my ultimate aim was to play a lead role in a big West End musical.

I was playing Cinderella in pantomime in Milton Keynes, and one day between shows I was getting a bite to eat in the shopping centre when my agent called me:

'Hello, darling. What are you up to?'

'Just between shows, grabbing food, why?'

'How would you feel about playing Galinda in *Wicked*?'

'Aaaaaaaaaaaargh! You're joking!!'

Then followed tears of joy, and a lot of screaming. To be offered such a fantastic role in one of the biggest musicals in the world was an overwhelming experience. I skipped onto stage as Cinderella that evening!

Wicked was a career-changing experience for me, and one I'll always remember and appreciate. Of course, returning to the show, this time playing Elphaba, was equally thrilling and in many ways even more so. Whilst playing Galinda, I would often wonder what it would be like to trade roles and defy gravity just once – but I never in a million years thought it would actually become a reality. Ten months after leaving the show I was at home one evening and received a call from Petra Siniawski, *Wicked*'s Associate Director in the West End. She told me that they had been auditioning all week and after a long day, the panel were chatting and my name popped up: 'Why isn't Lou being seen for Elphaba?'

The *Wicked* creative team had got to know me very well in the two years I had worked with them; they had seen my numerous concerts outside of the show; and they thought I was more than capable of playing Elphaba. Additionally, it would be an incredibly exciting cast announcement: never before had an actress played the roles of both Galinda and Elphaba. I had a long chat with Petra and agreed to go in the next day to audition. I was terrified as I felt there was such a lot riding on this; the team I respected so much had put their faith in me and I had to deliver!

The audition went very well and a couple of weeks later I got the call from my agent who said, 'Are you sitting down, Lou? They want you to play the green girl!' I remember walking out of my front door onto the green outside my house in pure shock! It was happening, I was going to play

Elphaba, the Wicked Witch of the West! That moment will stay with me for ever. I have the creative team of *Wicked* in London to thank for being so open-minded and thinking outside of the box. The show raised my profile and has opened so many doors. And I have the most wonderful group of fans from doing the show, who support me in everything I do.

Part Two

SECRETS OF GETTING A JOB

Auditioning and Agents

How do I get an audition for a professional show?

Before you can get a job, you have to get the audition in the first place – and that's not always as easy as performers would like it to be! The most common way to get an audition for professional work is through an agent. The producers putting on the show will almost certainly have employed a casting director, whose main responsibility is to coordinate the audition process and work alongside the creative team as they search for the right performers to cast.

The casting director will send out a casting breakdown to all of the agents they work with on a regular basis, often distributing it through Spotlight, the UK's main casting database. This breakdown will include all the details of the production – the title of the show, the producers, the creative team; the start dates of rehearsals, previews and performances; and so on – and will give a brief description of every character in the show or, for ensemble auditions, will describe what they are looking for more generally. Agents then propose any of their clients they consider appropriate, and then must wait to hear which of those clients the casting director invites to attend an audition.

How do I find out about open auditions?

Another option is looking out for open auditions. These are exactly as they sound: open for anyone and everyone to audition if they want to (as long as they fulfil the basic criteria of appearance, age and abilities). Unfortunately, these sorts of open auditions don't happen as often as they used to, but they do still exist.

New productions will occasionally hold open auditions, especially if they need to find a large cast with a real variety of people. The producers benefit in other ways too – they increase their chances of discovering more talent simply by seeing more people – but it can also prove excellent publicity for the eventual production.

The perfect example of this would be the casting for the 2013 West End revival of *A Chorus Line* which is (funnily enough!) a show about dancers auditioning for a production. The producers held weeks of private auditions, organised through casting directors and agents in the usual way, but in a case of life imitating art, they also held open auditions on stage at the London Palladium, where the production was scheduled to run.

The line of performers snaked around the entire building, with everyone standing in the cold for hours, all wearing numbers on their chests – much like what happens in the show itself. All of this was, of course, filmed and documented then released to the media. It proved to be the perfect footage to promote such an iconic show and sell a lot more tickets than if they had just kept the auditions private.

The most reliable source for finding out about open auditions is *The Stage*, the performing industry's weekly newspaper. (Aside from news, reviews, features, interviews and job adverts, *The Stage* also has a comprehensive and useful training section each week, which is definitely worth reading.) Since open auditions are held to get the maximum number of performers through the door, it makes sense for the producers to promote them as widely as possible.

Sometimes open auditions will take place outside of London, especially when performers with a specific regional accent are required, or – in the case of a show like *Billy Elliot* – the production team are dependent on discovering younger performers with particular skills. Local and regional theatres may put information about open auditions on their own websites, so keep an eye on these too.

I don't have an agent – and can't get one because I'm inexperienced. How can I find out about auditions?

When you're starting out in the industry there is an unavoidable Catch-22 situation, where you can't get a job because you don't have an agent, but you can't get an agent because they'll only take you on as client if they see you in a show and like your work. This is certainly a tricky situation and it can be frustrating, but there are always things you can do.

Any agent who is really worth having won't invest in you without seeing what you can do, so your priority should be to try and get a performing job without an agent. You can try writing directly to casting directors when you hear that productions are being announced. The sad reality is, though, that there are so many performers in competition already that often you'd need a unique or specialist set of skills to be considered. If you think a role or a production might suit you, then there is nothing to be lost by this route. You should also actively search for any open auditions that are happening (see the answer above for how to do this).

The best way to try and get an agent is to perform in a fringe production. Most of the time these are unpaid, but sometimes are on a profit-share basis, so that any money made by the production, above all the initial and running costs, is equally shared amongst the cast and production team at the end of the run. Even though the job is not very likely to end up making you any money at all, these can be good-quality, if small-scale, productions – and agents will often go to see potential clients in them. Increasingly, fringe work is reviewed, often very favourably, in the national press too.

Working on a smaller scale (and without paying performers) can mean that production companies can revive unusual or neglected work, push boundaries more frequently, and try new things, without commercial pressures or the astronomical budgets that are required to mount a show in the West End. Off-West End and fringe work can be enormously exciting, and one of the main avenues today that allows new writers, creatives and performers to create and develop their work, and start making a name for themselves.

Should I get an agent?

The answer to this question is undoubtedly 'Yes'! Some people can get work without an agent, but in this day and age, if you want a successful career we believe you will need to have a good agent, who will offer you all of the following (and more):

- They help find and then secure auditions for you.
- They gather constructive feedback for you during auditions.
- They negotiate a contractual deal on your behalf when you get offered work.
- They do a lot of behind-the-scenes work making sure the right people know who you are, and what you are up to.
- They encourage industry professionals to be interested in you and your work, and invite them to see you when you perform.

- They fight your corner if a company is in breach of contract.
- They offer support and guidance at all times and help you make difficult decisions about the development of your career.
- They are there to be the 'bad guy' who liaises with producers when necessary, so you only have to focus on performing.

Overall, a good agent will provide you with consistent and valuable support in an industry which is forever changing.

How can I get a role in a fringe production?

Many fringe theatres will do their casting in-house, so call them on the phone to see who to contact about auditions, especially if you hear of a show they are producing that you consider yourself right for. Instead of just emailing your CV and headshot to them, we would suggest going to the theatre, watching whichever show they have playing at that time, and, if appropriate, ask to see the person whose name you were given on the phone. Give your CV and headshot to them personally, and try to engage in a short conversation. This is when seeing the show at that theatre comes in useful, because it's an immediate topic for polite discussion – just don't say you hate it! Attach a letter to your CV 'introducing' yourself (so they remember who you are later on) and explaining that you'd like to be considered for their upcoming production. Make sure you have your contact information included somewhere clearly, and hopefully they will be in touch. Making an impression and being memorable when no one knows who you are is extremely important. You stand more of a chance of getting yourself an audition – and winning the job – by putting in this effort, as opposed just to mailing your CV.

As fringe productions rarely run longer than six weeks, the venue will be auditioning for their next show within a couple of months, so you should do everything you can to prepare well for your audition. This means that, even if you're not offered this role, you just might impress the producers enough to stay in their minds – and be invited back to audition next time around.

When you do get a job (keep faith!), make a list of the agents you would like to meet and invite them to see your show. This will involve providing them with a complimentary ticket, plus one for their guest – which unfortunately you will probably have to pay for yourself! Although you'll want to contact as many agents as possible to stand a better chance of securing one to represent you, if you invite ten agents and they all agree to come, that's potentially twenty tickets, which could become very expensive considering you're working for free.

I worked on a profit-share show in 2009 called *Jet Set Go!*, an original British musical written by Jake Brunger and Pippa Cleary. I played a gay flight attendant named Richard whose only real ambition was to fall in love with the perfect guy. The great thing about this job was that everyone involved was so enthusiastic because we were clearly there just to be working on something fulfilling. We were all working other jobs at the same time to pay the rent, but we thoroughly enjoyed the three-week run at the Jermyn Street Theatre in London. When we finished, we did actually receive a share of the profits: £206 each (for a five-week job). The money was such a massive bonus and we were so grateful, as we'd expected to make nothing at all. It's so nice when theatre doesn't have to be about the money.

Although I have never worked on a profit-share production before, I have sought to gain experience with new writers and musical directors – and get additional exposure – by recording albums, on a free or profit-share basis. Whether it's a new musical or a collection of new songs, or just being part of an album alongside other up-and-coming singers in the industry, this experience may not earn you any money but it gets your voice heard, and the recording is something you can send to a prospective agent. It's another approach that can work, and once again shows that sometimes you have to be prepared to work for little or no money to advance your career in the long run.

How should I find and select an agent?

Contacts is a handbook published by Spotlight that features listing information for most UK agents (as well as photographers, casting directors, acting classes, rehearsal spaces, and so on). It will provide you with information about agents, their contact details, and website addresses; then you can look online to see which agents represent the performers you admire, respect and who are doing the sort of work that you would like to do. Start by contacting these ones.

Most agents will want to see potential clients perform – so invite them to your drama-school productions or showcase, if you are still in training, or to a fringe/profit-share production, if possible (see the answer above for more information about these productions).

When you don't have representation it can seem like the first thing you want and need to kick-start your career. But we would strongly advise you not to make any rash judgements or decisions. Make sure that you meet potential agents and talk to them properly, see how comfortable you feel with them, what sort of jobs they realistically think they can help you win, and what they believe they can offer you. Remember that an agent works for *you* – it's your commission they take (generally 10–15% of your earnings), not the other way round – you have to be on the same page so you can develop a good working relationship. You might find that a larger agency isn't right for you, as you might feel overlooked in favour of many of the other actors on their books; alternatively, you might find a smaller, boutique agency doesn't have the same clout overall. It's a very personal thing, finding the right agent, and some performers go through many over the years.

Once you've got work, agents will negotiate the terms and conditions of your contract as well, hopefully guaranteeing the best deal for you. There's not much room for manoeuvre though, since the actors' union Equity has agreed fixed rates that theatre producers and production companies must pay the performers in their productions. At the time of writing, the minimum that West End performers must be paid is £518–633 per week, depending on the size of venue.

I have been with the same agent throughout my entire career. I contacted Michael Garrett at Global Artists when I was touring in *Grease*. We met up and instantly I felt comfortable with him; he was honest, telling me what direction he felt I should move in and agreeing to take me on because I already had a job. This meant there was already something that he could see me in, and he could invite other industry people (casting directors, producers, etc.) to see me in. At the time, it was a very small agency – but has grown tremendously over the last fifteen years. Even though it's changed in size, I have remained there because I still feel that the entire team understand what I want from my career, they know me well personally, we have a mutual respect and a great relationship. I can be honest with them, talking openly if I don't feel comfortable with something, and I trust them to help me make the right decisions. Here's what Michael Garrett said when I asked him what he's looking for in a performer:

> I am always searching for the principal player, but more importantly the artist that has the talent to become the principal player. Foremost I'm seeking the 'actor', then beyond this, the triple threat: the actor that can also sing and dance. Next I look for the artist to have a truthful and

confident perception of his or her own talent and, crucially, his or her limitations. And finally, I must feel that not only do I want to work with the actor, but that other industry professionals from all forums will also – not just for one engagement, but again and again.

Mark Ward of Belfield and Ward Agency has represented me professionally since I graduated from college. He and Phil Belfield, together with my manager Rebecca Sichel-Coates, have helped guide me through my career over the past ten years, making crucial decisions and bold choices to enable me to achieve success. Even though I'm now living in the US, I still have very close relationships with all of them; in fact, they helped introduce me to my new agents in New York City.

During my first six months touring with *The Book of Mormon*, I drove from Boston to New York City for a couple of days to have some general meetings with casting directors, to discover how they thought I could make the most of opportunities in the US. During these days, I met with a manager, Vikram Dhawer; we got on really well, and I liked his perspective on the industry. He even flew to Toronto to see me in *Mormon*, and I ended up signing with him as his client. Vikram then arranged meetings for me with four great bi-coastal agencies (with offices in both Los Angeles and New York), and I ultimately decided to sign with Paradigm, a fantastic talent agency.

Regardless of where you are in your career, there is always a process in getting an agent, one that takes time and must be carefully considered and negotiated. It should not be a daunting thing; look on it as a process that you need to go through – and one that can be exciting. Believe in yourself as a product that agents or managers will be fortunate to represent. This confidence will come across when you meet them, and might convince them that you're the sort of performer who will get jobs – and ultimately this is what will make them want to represent you.

What happens at an audition?

Every single audition is different, but we can give you a flavour of what they can be like and the process you'll go through.

First of all, you'll get your audition (or 'call') time from your agent, or maybe directly from the casting director. When you arrive on the day (and on time!), there will be a person signing you in or just a sign-in sheet for you to write your name on. Sometimes the audition venue will feel very relaxed, and you'll arrive to a virtually empty waiting area, where maybe two or three other people are waiting to audition. Other times you'll arrive and be greeted by a room crammed full of people warming up, doing their hair and make-up, and a very tense, competitive energy buzzing around the room.

What we advise that you do is the same in each and every scenario you are met with. Before you walk into the audition venue, take a couple of deep breaths and focus on the job at hand. You are there for you and nobody else, so it really doesn't matter what anybody else's routine is, how they prepare or how they conduct themselves in that environment. Don't get dragged into any potentially controversial conversations or rumours about the show you are auditioning for. Find a quiet space to get yourself ready, prepared and focused, and then you'll enter the audition room feeling as in control as possible.

If it's a dance audition, you will be going in the room with a group of people, anything from three or four to fifty, depending on the situation and what you're auditioning for. You will learn a dance routine as one big group, then you'll be separated into smaller groups of usually three to five people at a time and you'll perform the routine a couple of times. Bear in mind that, although this is your moment to shine and perform, there are eyes on you from the second you walk into the room, watching how quickly you can pick up the steps, what you look like, your attention to detail, how you take adjustments or direction, and so on. And there might be a lot of eyes. A big musical might have up to twenty creatives, producers, casting directors and assistants, sitting there watching and passing judgement on you.

At the end of the dance call, the casting panel will either let everyone leave the room, and they will contact your agent later if you have a recall, or they will announce the successful actors then and there, and thank everyone else for attending. Then the audition will move on to singing, either the same day, or another day, when you'll perform the songs you've been asked to prepare. And then possibly a reading – where you'll act some scenes – if you're going for a featured role, or to understudy one.

For your singing audition, make sure you have the songs completely prepared. Usually the first time you sing for the panel (particularly for ensemble auditions) you will take in your own song, or songs, to perform. Take your music to the pianist, take the time to explain any edits so they understand, give them the tempo you want to take the song at, and any other information they need to know, so they can be as accurate as possible.

A short time after the first round of auditions, you will be told, probably via your agent, if you are being invited for a recall. Most of the time, you'll be expected to prepare something else – generally a scene or a song from the show you're auditioning for. The recall could be the next day, which doesn't give you long to learn it!

I used to attend auditions like this all the time, with my prepared songs and speeches, when I was auditioning for ensemble roles at the beginning of my career. The more I started to play lead roles, it would be more likely that I would be sent the material of the part I was auditioning for. This can be great, because you can instantly show the audition panel what you might do with the role; on the other hand, if you walk in and the director thinks you just don't look right, you've wasted a lot of time and effort learning what can sometimes be up to six songs and just as many scenes. But it's all part of the process. Once I went through thirteen rounds of auditions for one show, which felt crazy. Thankfully, I did end up getting the job; if I hadn't, I'd have been one very frustrated little Welshman!

What happens at an open audition?

If you're going to an open audition, you should arrive at the audition venue at least an hour before the registration time so that you can be one of the first people to be seen; otherwise you could be there all day. Generally, you register upon arrival. Make sure you take your up-to-date CV and a high-quality headshot to give to the casting team. You will be given a number (to wear when you're actually in the audition room) and a specific time to come back to audition during that day. The earlier you register, the sooner you'll be auditioned.

If the show requires dancing, there will usually be the dance audition first, as it's the fastest way to sift through those who can actually do what's required, and those who can't. There will probably be a few cuts during the audition – where you are told if you have or haven't made it, and if you're required to stay at the audition longer. If 'cut' sounds like a painful term, then the rejection can feel like that too, but try not to take it personally.

If you are kept through to the final dance round, you'll probably be asked to sing as well. You must have sheet music with you which is edited clearly and taped together in the correct order so that it's easy for the pianist to sight-read. Ensure that you have the number and styles of songs requested. If you make it through the singing audition, you'll often be invited to join the remaining private auditions that are scheduled for the rest of the casting period.

I've never been to an open audition for a musical, but when I was sixteen my sister and her husband drove me to Manchester for an open audition for a boy band called Boysterous – at that point all I wanted was to be in a pop group. I had planned on singing 'My Love' by Westlife for the audition, and had rehearsed it so many times and felt well prepared. We arrived at the venue and the line of young guys waiting to get into the building was ridiculously long. Everyone wanted to be part of Boysterous, apparently. After waiting in line for hours, I eventually walked into the building, but I didn't even get to sing. I was told that I was too fat, didn't look right and was asked to leave. Harsh! So I left, a little disheartened, having not sung a note, and took my sixteen-year-old self off to eat a doughnut!

I got the role of Jan in *Grease* from an open audition. I was relatively unknown at that stage and it was very early on in my career. My agent couldn't get me seen for the musical in a private audition so, knowing I was perfect for the show,

I went along to an open audition. It was exactly how you would imagine: literally hundreds of people queuing up outside. I finally got into the building and was given a number to pin to my top. More waiting for hours, getting more and more nervous, and then I was finally called in to learn the dance routine. This is where my dance training came in handy because had I not got through that dance call, I'd never have had the chance to sing for the panel, which is what won me the role of Jan. Don't ever think 'It's not worth going to an open audition!'

How should I prepare for an audition?

We've learned that the more auditions you do, the better you get at dealing with them and the easier they become. Having to audition is something that can be very nerve-racking, intense and sometimes downright humiliating – but for every time we've stepped foot into an audition and come out thinking it went badly, we have learned something invaluable from that experience. You have to accept that auditioning is something all performers do – even the biggest Hollywood movie stars will quite often have to screen test or audition for a role – so you need to train yourself not to fear them and to find a way of becoming good at them.

You should prepare as much as you possibly can. Research the production, the show, its writers and the creative team. Google is a wonderful thing. If you are asked to prepare some of the script, learn it until it's as if you wrote it yourself. If you are sent a song, don't just learn the melody –

sing it through so often that it fits your voice and you can do it justice. If you have a dance audition, make sure you've warmed up, you're wearing the correct attire, and are focused as soon as you step into that room.

We honestly believe that you cannot prepare too much for an audition. You can certainly over-analyse your preparation and your material, and let things eat away at your self-esteem and confidence, but the more prepared you are, the more confident you will be and the less painful the experience of auditioning will be. You need to give yourself the best chance to do 'you' justice.

I am constantly finding things that inspire me in my life and career. Some of the best audition advice I've ever heard was from Bryan Cranston, the amazing American actor who plays Walter White in *Breaking Bad*, and it can be seen in the YouTube video: 'Bryan Cranston's Advice to Aspiring Performers'. He basically explains how he hit a turning point in his career eighteen years ago when he realised that he was going into auditions trying to get a job instead of walking in there and using that time to just 'create a compelling and interesting character, that serves the text, presenting it within the environment where the audition happens and then walking away'. It's so simple but so very useful to think like this before stepping into an audition. Let's not worry about the end result or fixate on trying to get a job. Let's just do what we do best – and act!

How do I choose monologues for auditioning?

A monologue is a scripted speech that is performed by a solo actor. When auditioning for drama school or for jobs in theatre, TV or film, you will sometimes be asked to perform a monologue of your own choosing.

There are many monologue books available in shops that are full of a variety of classical and contemporary acting pieces. You may find them useful, especially if you don't have access to many playscripts in your local bookshops and library. They can act like a springboard and give you ideas of other characters or plays or playwrights to explore. But, if you do use them, do so very carefully! Often the selection of pieces is quite random and varied, containing a whole range of accents, ages and types of characters. How can you possibly perform a monologue that's written for a twenty-year-old Irish girl and another for a sixty-year-old woman from London? No one is that versatile. Also, the choices in these anthologies can be overused by auditionees – especially for drama-school auditions – so if you want to stand out from the crowd, you should look in other places for your monologues.

One idea would be to make a list of your favourite performers, or those you think you are similar to, then to find out which plays or films they've been in. Locate the script for these plays (or write the speeches down from watching the DVD) and see if these monologues suit you too. Don't use anything too familiar, or just copy the actor's performance, because you'll just be compared to the original actor and it will seem like you're doing an impersonation rather than acting. You should also read as many plays as you can, especially those by writers you like or relate to. Find out what other work they've done and jot down any potential monologues from those pieces.

A monologue doesn't have to be long. A lot of people assume they need to be wordy and a page or two long, but one minute is long enough for most auditions – and that time flies once you start acting. The best thing to look for is a character that you can portray – something that is not too dissimilar to you in terms of age, appearance or accent. Think if you could realistically be cast as the character; if the answer's no, then it's probably a dangerous audition speech to choose. If you can realistically see yourself as the character, then it's the better choice. The audition panel want to see what you look like, what you sound like and if you can create a believable character – it's easier for them to see these things if you perform a piece which is within your range and your abilities.

How do I choose songs for auditioning?

Many people have their set audition songs, and go from audition to audition singing the same ones whether they are appropriate or not. One performer we know has a song portfolio that consists of 'Mr Cellophane' from *Chicago* – and that's it! He is not a confident singer so this song is his one option, because it's not too demanding, and sticks within a very small vocal range. But how do you think the panel of a big rock musical – *We Will Rock You* or *Jesus Christ Superstar*, for instance – would react to you telling them you're going to sing 'Mr Cellophane', when the brief they gave your agent was that you should bring two contrasting rock songs that show off your range and style?!

Personally I don't have one audition folder, but a box full of folders each containing audition songs in the following sort of categories:

- Musical-theatre Ballads
- Musical-theatre Uptempo
- Contemporary Musical Theatre
- Classic Musicals (e.g. 1940/50s)
- Pop Songs

This means I can go straight to the folder and have lots of options. Of course there are a few favourites I always pull out, but I try to vary what I use to keep it interesting for myself and the panel, who may have seen and heard me before.

My singing portfolio is huge. I have so many songs in there, but I realised a few years back that I couldn't possibly memorise hundreds of songs and be able to perform them to the standard required at the drop of a hat. Now I probably only use about ten that I take to every audition; they're a real variety of songs and I'm confident with all of them. If I'm required to sing something very specific, I know I probably have something appropriate within my entire portfolio somewhere, but will just need to brush up on it a little.

When auditioning for a role, should I look at other people who have previously played the same role?

I don't think I have ever actively looked to see who has played a role before me – but that's generally because I already know since the shows I've auditioned for have been pretty high-profile. I knew the guys who preceded me in *Wicked, Ghost* and *The Book of Mormon*, because those shows are always announcing cast changes, and most of the time they're friends or people I know within the industry. But it's never a good idea to compare yourself to or try to copy someone else's performance.

I have looked to see who's played a role before me, but just to see if I am similar and whether the casting team always go for a similar look or whether they are open to variety. Don't ever try to imitate anyone. Always bring something new to the table.

What should I do on the day of an audition?

Everyone has a different routine, and you'll develop your own, but these are our top tips for the day of an audition, and what you might find when you're there.

- The night before your audition, get everything ready and prepared: your outfit (what you'll wear, plus any other equipment, your jazz shoes or knee pads, etc.), your sheet music and your script. Plan your journey to the audition venue. There is nothing worse than leaving it until the last minute, getting lost and being late.
- Wake up and get out of bed in good time, having had a good night's sleep before. It always helps.
- Eat a good breakfast – but make it fairly light. Being nervous on a full stomach isn't much fun. Aim to have foods that will release energy slowly, such as oatmeal or porridge, a handful of nuts, and some fruit (a banana or berries). Don't have any dairy products as they will affect your voice; and drink plenty of water. Take a bottle of water and snacks with you to the audition in case you need a little boost of energy.
- Do a vocal warm-up if you're going to sing or even just speak in the audition. A gentle vocal warm-up whilst you are getting ready will ensure you don't arrive completely cold. Then when you arrive at the venue, find a quiet space to warm up properly and maybe run through your songs. You'll rarely get a physical warm-up for a dance call, so it's up to you to stretch your body to avoid injury.

- Try taking a long walk if it's an important meeting – like a final audition for the directors and producers – to clear your head and focus your thoughts.
- Make sure you arrive at the audition venue about twenty minutes before your appointment. Arrive earlier than that and you'll be surrounded by other actors preparing, which can be distracting; arrive any later, and you'll be feeling flustered and rushed before entering the room. On rare occasions the panel will be running ahead of schedule too, so it's good to be there with a few minutes to prepare for whatever situation you have to face.
- Be polite – to everyone in the venue. It's basic manners and courtesy, but also you never know what connection they have with the production team. Sometimes the person calling your name out at the door can be asked for their opinion on you. Moaning in the waiting area is not a good start.
- Regarding your attitude on the day of your audition, you should always be yourself. Genuine, happy people work more. Keep focused and professional. Be confident in your talent and what you could bring to the show. Treat every audition as an experience and don't pin all your hopes on the one role. You won't win every one you audition for. And finally, do your very best. No one expects anything more than that.

How should I interact with other actors at auditions?

It's difficult before an audition when you're in a confined space, face to face with many of the other people going for the same job as you.

Some other actors will be chatty and ask you lots of questions about your audition process thus far, perhaps to work out what's going to happen for them in their audition that day. Others will play it cool about the audition or the job, when in reality their palms are sweating and they feel threatened by every other person within the building at that time. A few people will do their best to drop loud comments about the positive feedback they've had from the panel in previous rounds of auditions, or how they've worked for the choreographer four times in the past as an attempt to feel superior and make everyone else feel threatened.

There's often an actor who knows everybody and talks loudly to the whole room in general about mutual friends and 'what they've been up to'. And there will be the quiet people who just sit studying their material in the corner. That's the approach we prefer to take. We think it's advisable to cut out all the insecure, chattering nonsense and just take time to prepare, keeping yourself to yourself. Think about what you want to achieve with your character, but keeping your thoughts open and responsive so that you are ready to take direction in the audition room.

How do I get past feelings of doubt and nervousness when auditioning?

Every performer endures those inner demons that are constantly filling your head with feelings of doubt, and fuelling a lack of confidence. Believe it or not, there is a way to combat those inner demons! It simply involves focusing your mind and energy on a more positive outlook.

First of all, strip away all those unnecessary thoughts you think before auditions: 'I'm not as good as the person who came out of the room before me', 'I need this job to pay my rent', 'My voice feels scratchy and I'm anxious about those high notes'... All performers have insecurities and so we have to learn to live with them and not let them get the better of us.

None of us knows exactly what the audition panel are looking for, so even if the person who is in the room before you is naturally more talented than you, you may look more appropriate or have the right sound. Even in a long-running show, the creative team might decide to 'make this new cast a bit younger' or they know that 'our new leading man is 6'5" so our leading lady needs to be taller than usual'. You should never anticipate what might happen in the room, or what they are looking for. You can't predict the future in real life so you shouldn't attempt to do it with auditions. All you do know is that they are wanting and needing to find the right person, who can do the job, and matches the requirements of the role. They want you to succeed, so concentrate on trying to give them the best that you can do. If you're not right for them, then that's not necessarily anything to do with you or your talent – you just might not be right.

Make a list of all the things that are great about yourself. There's no room for modesty; no one else needs to see this list so just go for gold and inflate your ego. You can include anything and everything on that list as long as it's a positive. Here's an example:

- I have a great smile.
- I have an excellent vocal range.
- I am funny.
- My hair looks great.
- My CV is looking good.
- I have a very supportive family.
- I am a hardworking person.
- I am generous.

The qualities you write down don't need to be industry-related; just start with positive thoughts and then you'll think of more and more things to write about until you realise that YOU ARE A GREAT PERSON and the production team would benefit greatly from working with you. Just be careful you don't cross the fine line into being arrogant and egotistical, or writing down the characteristics you would *like* to have, rather than those that you actually do. These thoughts should be held like a quiet fire inside of you, burning just enough to get you through whatever you need to in a confident, assured way.

You should also do your homework as much as possible to help you feel comfortable and confident before, during and after your audition. Make sure you learn that scene or rehearse that song or practise the dance routine you were taught at the previous audition, because if you prepare properly you give yourself the best possible chance of success.

When auditioning, are there any things that I definitely should be mentioning or talking about – and things that I shouldn't?

Keep the conversation polite and generic. If it's a long-running show, don't ask questions about the details of who is leaving the show or being replaced. Focus on what you are doing there and then in the room. Take your time and don't try too hard!

I have one big regret: at my second audition for *Ghost*, I met Matthew Warchus, the director of the show (and now the Artistic Director of the Old Vic). He asked me if I had seen the show and I thought it would be funny (in my head) to say, 'Yeah I did, and yeah, it was pretty good, I s'pose' – as if I wasn't that fussed about it, forgetting that they weren't aware of just how much I loved the show and really wanted to be in it. I mean, I saw it and immediately bought a guitar so I could audition for it. Instead, I must have come across as if I just didn't give a damn whether I got the job or not – and a creative team, who invest so much time, effort and money into a project, want and need to feel like the actors auditioning also want to be part of it.

Will Burton, *Ghost*'s casting director, called my agent saying, 'Mark is doing really well for this, and they're seriously interested in him for it, but he did seem a bit like he wasn't bothered about doing the show.' My agent's response was 'Are you kidding? Mark's been calling me daily to make sure I get him an audition for this. Believe me, he wants this job!' My stupid comment clearly hasn't remained a big regret because I got the job in the end, but I will never forget the first impression I made by trying to act the cool guy!

What will make me stand out in an audition?

The things that will make you stand out in an audition are largely out of your control, apart from the obvious things like wearing something outrageous or dying your hair bright green. (Both of which are to be avoided!) Generally, people focus too much on standing out and being noticed, instead of trusting that the creative team making the casting decisions will have a vision. If you fit that vision they will see it in you and investigate it further.

We have been in auditions where people deliberately trip up as they leave the audition room – so they'll be remembered as 'the one who fell over on their way out'. Do you really want to be remembered for that?!

Instead, focus on letting your talent, your preparation, your professionalism and your personality shine out. Have faith that the audition panel will find what they need to, if you have what they're looking for.

How do I progress from the ensemble to a leading role?

If you take a look at how many musicals there are and how many people there are in their casts, it's clear that there are far more ensemble roles than there are leading roles. As a result, there are far fewer jobs available for leading actors, so getting your first leading role may take a long time, lots of understudying and starting off in the ensemble. It takes time to build up your CV and show that you are experienced enough to deal with the pressure of a leading role. There are many people who get their break early, for some it takes a while and others, as much as they would love a leading role and are very talented, never get that break at all. Once a performer has played a few leading roles, it becomes easier for them to play leading roles in other musicals, because they have the experience, the talent, the reputation and the fan base that producers look for when they're casting.

We both believe that it is important to work your way up the ladder when it comes to the roles you play – and we were both in the ensemble and understudied roles before we got lead roles in our own right. You learn so much from being in the ensemble, and especially from being a swing, where you understudy six or seven ensemble roles. If someone can't perform – because of injury, illness, holiday or an emergency – then the swing steps in to save the day. It's enormously difficult keeping so many roles in your head at once, requiring a lot of talent, intelligence and organisation. It's an experience that benefits any performer.

You should be like a sponge in any job you get: watch what is going on around you, how the director works, and what the leading performers possess that makes them successful. It's about much more than just talent – often leading performers have a presence, charisma and confidence that marks them out. Ask questions, don't be afraid to speak up, find out as much as you can about the industry, and discover what you can do to improve (and there's room for improvement in everyone). If opportunities come up to audition for the understudy of a role, speak to your director or choreographer and ask to be considered. Be patient. If it's meant to happen, your opportunity will come; don't be in a rush to have everything handed to you straight away. It's valuable to appreciate how hard it is to achieve your dream of playing leading roles, so that when you get there you have a real sense of pride and achievement. There is nothing wrong with being passionate and determined, but you should also always be humble and grateful.

When I graduated from Laine Theatre Arts I was lucky enough to go straight into a lead role in a musical, the Narrator in the UK tour of *Joseph and the Amazing Technicolor Dreamcoat*. As I've mentioned, I had been in the choir in the same show when I was a child, so it was a dream role. This was a scaled-down version of the musical, so we used to do twelve shows a week – two shows every single day, six days a week! It was such hard work but it taught me such discipline. I had to look after myself and my voice as best I could, so absolutely no partying or staying up late. I used a steam inhaler to help my voice every morning and every night, and did warm-ups before every show. After *Joseph* I joined the UK tour of *Grease* in the smaller role of Jan, one of the Pink Ladies. Of course I wanted to continue playing lead roles but the next job I actually took was as a swing in the musical *Kiss Me, Kate*.

After *Kiss Me, Kate* I played some other lead roles in shows such as *Jekyll and Hyde, Debbie Does Dallas* and *Cinderella*. Then it was back to being in the ensemble. I made the decision to understudy again because of the particular show, director and production company. I felt it would be such a wonderful opportunity to work with those people even if it meant going back to being in the ensemble and understudying. It was the right decision because the following year I was offered the lead role I had understudied, Sarah Brown in *Guys and Dolls*. A truly remarkable experience and one that taught me so much as an actress. After that I played Evita and then got the role of Galinda in *Wicked*, which led me to return to Oz and play Elphaba. My career has been a slow, steady climb up the ladder – every new role was a stepping stone to the next one – and I look back with huge pride and a sense of achievement.

How do I avoid being typecast?

Typecasting is when a particular actor becomes strongly identified with a specific type of character or characters, with the same traits, similar personalities or from the same social or ethnic groups – and then finds it hard to get work playing other types of characters because they have been 'pigeonholed' as that certain type. Sometimes the performer is happy to go along with always getting offered the same sort of role, because it means getting work and having a successful career. Maybe they don't particularly want to try and change in order to open up different doors and opportunities. Sometimes, though, it can be incredibly frustrating for an actor who would love new challenges.

If you have a very strong look when you go into an audition (maybe you're kooky, or nerdy, or ultra-hip…), then you might be forcing yourself into being typecast. Try a more neutral look, so that you are more of a blank canvas, easily adaptable for whatever role you are auditioning for. If you start going down a road where you are accepting similar roles and you don't feel satisfied doing this, then you have a decision to make. You may have to be brave and turn a couple of roles down in order to be seen differently, but this is obviously hard, as you will want to keep working, especially if it's early in your career.

Alternatively, take the roles and build up a good CV, meet and work with directors and choreographers, and wait a while before you make the decision about where you'd like your career to go. There are many incredibly successful actors who are always typecast, but because they are so talented in that particular field and enjoy it, they are happy to stay there. Very often, comedy or character actors constantly get cast in comedy roles, which isn't a bad thing necessarily – but look at the famous actors who manage to cross over and perform both comedy and drama, and imagine how fulfilling that must be.

After I had played the comic role of Jan in *Grease*, I was offered the role of Mabel in the musical *Fame*. These roles are similar in that they are both American girls, they are both comedy roles that require the actor to be a little chubby, and they both get teased about eating too much food at times. I took the decision there and then that, even though I knew I'd have a lot of fun playing Mabel, I didn't want to play such a similar role so soon, so I turned the job down. It was scary but felt like the right thing to do at the time.

I've always enjoyed singing big beautiful ballads and, although I love comedy, I wanted my next role to be a straight, dramatic one. I looked at why I was being offered these roles and decided to eat a healthy diet, do some exercise and lose a little weight, which I did. This led to me getting cast in *Kiss Me, Kate* and then a dream role of mine in *Jekyll and Hyde*, Lucy Harris. Sometimes you have to be prepared to take action and adjust how you look in order to achieve your goals.

When I moved to New York City, I deliberately took a break from my career for about six months, and instead focused on getting back into classes and coaching in order to fine-tune my skills and figure out exactly what I wanted in my life and my career. During this time in classes we talked a lot about our 'type' – up until this point I had played the romantic lead in most of the jobs I'd done; usually a stereotypical 'tall, dark, handsome dude'. And so that was the material I would take to work on in classes, even though it wasn't especially fulfilling or challenging after ten years of doing those roles.

In group discussions, other actors would suggest much darker, more mature, more sinister types of roles and characters for me to try. I'd gone from being the boyfriend, the American high-school jock, and the romantic conflicted guy, to being the villain, the lawyer, the murderer, the young dad, the psycho, the vindictive husband...! Basically, I became very excited because I realised that I didn't have to feel stuck in the same type. I had gotten older, as we all do, and with that ageing came a shift in my casting potential. I have embraced it with open arms and have been auditioning for and doing jobs where I don't always have to play the good guy. Sometimes we need to embrace our typecasting and not resist it, especially if it means we get work. But there will come a time when, naturally, things start to shift. I may possibly be the only person in the world who's excited about ageing, but I really don't think it needs to be a concern when the goal is to have longevity and a nourishing, progressive career.

How do I deal with rejection?

Lots and lots of people asked us this question, or variations on its theme, so it's obviously a big concern for a lot of people of all ages and with all ranges of experience. And unfortunately, the short answer is that you're going to have to face rejection – sometimes a lot. And it's particularly painful if it's a job you really wanted.

When I was younger and new to the industry, I would literally cry my eyes out when I got turned down for a job. I took it as a personal insult and always felt bad for days afterwards. Now, with more experience and understanding, I can appreciate the reasons and accept them more easily. It's still a dent to the ego, but I deal with it better.

Recently I auditioned for a play in the West End – straight acting is something I would love to do in the future – and got through to the final rounds. My feedback from the panel was great and gave me such confidence, but probably in hindsight gave me a false sense of security. I didn't get the role and, for the first time in a long time, I felt really upset about it. We are all in the business because we love it, so of course it hurts when something doesn't become a reality – but remember there is always something else around the corner. Dwelling on the 'whys' and 'why nots' won't help you to get the next job.

The biggest rejection I ever faced was undoubtedly the final result of the television show, *Eurovision: Your Country Needs You*. The UK's 2009 entry for the Eurovision Song Contest was decided by the public vote, and week after week the tension had been building up and the remaining contestants whittled down. Being voted out in third place was the greatest disappointment of my career, and it was all broadcast live to the nation, and immortalised for ever on YouTube, if you fancy watching it! You can see me willing Graham Norton, the host, not to say my name ('Don't say Mark, don't say Mark!') and, after an excruciatingly long pause… he does. I didn't do a very good job of hiding my disappointment. It took me several weeks to recover my confidence, and it was affecting the auditions I was doing, but after a few months I came to the realisation that actually it was the best thing that could have happened. Being on that TV show raised my profile enormously, and I began to be considered for leading roles. A year after my Eurovision rejection, I was touring as Brad Majors in *The Rocky Horror Show*, and on one single day, I got offered the lead in a West End musical, the lead in a touring musical, and the lead in an opera for a very respectable company.

Dealing with any sort of rejection or disappointment is all about your frame of mind, and how you handle it. If you allow yourself to feel unwanted, then you'll begin to hate yourself, your fellow performers, the industry and everything about it. You have to see each audition as an opportunity to make an impression and to show people what you can do. If it doesn't work out, then it's not the job for you. But hopefully there will be a project on the horizon that you're perfect for, and everything will fall into place. Have faith in yourself.

Anyone who knows me knows that one of my ultimate goals has been to perform my own show at the Royal Albert Hall in London. So when I was asked to be one of Michael Ball's guests on his UK tour which would play – guess where?! – the Royal Albert Hall, I couldn't believe my luck! It was so thrilling and something I will remember for ever.

Michael said to me that night: 'Take a picture in your mind.' Which is exactly what I did. When I walked out onto the stage and the music started, I took a moment to look out and take in the room. Over five thousand people were out there watching us that night, literally surrounding the stage. The wonderful dome shape of the roof in the Royal Albert Hall is spectacular, and for such a vast auditorium it feels strangely intimate when you're on stage. I've had the pleasure of performing there since – and each time is as special as the last.

My audition process for *Ghost: The Musical* in the West End was very quick. I met the associate creative team on a Friday morning, then they asked me return later that day to meet the director Matthew Warchus and producer Colin Ingram. I was sent a song to learn over the weekend (which happened to be the weekend of my debut album launch party, so I didn't have much study time!), and then on the Monday morning I was reading opposite two potential leading ladies for my final audition.

Later, my agent called me and said, 'They were extremely happy with what you did in the auditions, and they are very interested in you. But unfortunately they don't know if the role is even available at this stage because they are trying to piece together the casting puzzle between the London and New York productions, and a lot depends on visa issues, the legalities and so on… So for now, let's try to forget about it and then if something comes of it we'll discuss that if it happens – but well done!'

When you're waiting to hear if you've got a job, the suspense can drive you insane, so I genuinely convinced myself there was no job available, and just happily continued with my life, enjoying my final couple of months in *Wicked*.

Three weeks later, when I'd forgotten about *Ghost* altogether, my agent called me, and before I could even say hello, he began:

'Where are you?'

'I'm on the Tube to Fulham,' I replied, 'to visit my friend Amy on her lunch break from rehearsals.'

'Can you come meet me in half an hour?'

'Well, no, like I said, I'm meeting Amy. I could come and see you afterwards.'

'No, I'm watching a client in the *Legally Blonde* matinee. Can I see you after that?'

'Erm… yeah, I suppose. Is everything okay?'

'Yes, I just want to talk to you about something in person instead of over the phone.'

'Okay, can I know what it's about?'

'No. I'll meet you in Victoria for a coffee before your warm-up.'

Click!

So there I am, sitting on the Tube to Fulham thinking what the hell could it be, and after chatting to Amy over lunch we decided it was either that he was getting rid of me as a client *or* that I was going to get a job offer for *Ghost*. It was a very long five-hour wait to meet him, and I even had a forty-minute shower in my dressing room to kill time. He eventually met me in a café at 6 p.m., by which point I'd had to buy a herbal remedy to calm my nerves. I'd even bought his coffee before he arrived in order not to waste any more time. Finally, he turned up, sat down and began:

'So, *Legally Blonde* was in great shape.'

'Aaaaaagh! Are you seriously going to talk about *Legally Blonde* after keeping me waiting all afternoon?!'

He laughed.

'Okay okay. Well, as an agent there are certain conversations that cannot be had over the phone and one of the perks of my job is being able to have moments like this with my clients. I am so happy to tell you that this morning we had a phone call offering you the role of Sam Wheat in *Ghost: The Musical*. You start rehearsals in two weeks and you open on 13 January. Congratulations!'

The rest of the conversation cannot be printed because it involves far too much swearing. But I wept tears of joy and burned my hand by throwing green tea all over the table, so exhilarated I felt. I had worked so hard to win the role, and it's not that often in this industry that you truly get what you want. I still hate my agent for keeping me waiting all afternoon, but I wouldn't have had him tell me in any other way. It was very special.

Part Three

SECRETS OF DOING THE JOB

Rehearsing and Performing

What is the best way to approach a new role?

Your approach to a new role will very much depend on the demands of the role in question, and the opportunities and resources available to you.

Whenever we get a role in a large musical-theatre production, we begin with singing lessons to start singing the music into our instruments – our bodies and voices – as soon as possible. If there is going to be a heavy demand on our speaking voices with lots of dialogue, we would work with a vocal coach on supporting the text with our breathing and our physicality, so we can sustain a rigorous performing schedule without ruining our voices. And if we know we're going to be dancing a lot, we might take some classes so our bodies get used to the physical exhaustion – and don't get shocked during the rehearsal period and suffer injuries.

If you're at school, or performing in an amateur production, then taking some of these additional classes may not be possible for you, but you may have teachers or other members of the company who have experience in different areas. You can certainly do physical and vocal exercises every day to start limbering up your own instrument, and there are many books and DVDs which will guide you through keeping your voice supple and supported. If the show demands your physique needs to alter, you can go to the gym or work with a personal trainer.

Other than preparing your body, you should do as much research as possible – study the period the production is set in, read the novel that it's adapted from, work out the inspiration for telling this story now. Prepare some ideas about the character – who are they, what do they do, their interests, their ambitions, etc. – but don't have anything too fixed in your mind, in case the director disagrees! Study your script in great detail, so you can understand exactly what the writer (or writers) are trying to create with your character.

If there are specific skills you need to learn – for example, walking a tightrope, playing the violin, speaking French – begin training in whatever way you can to be ahead of the game before rehearsals begin.

What happens during a typical day of rehearsals?

Depending on the type of production, the rehearsal process can be anything from a few days to many weeks. A new musical opening in the West End would generally rehearse for four weeks in a studio; a week or two of technical rehearsals on stage, during which all the technical elements are incorporated; a preview period of a week or two, when changes might be made on a daily basis; before an official opening night.

A typical day in the rehearsal studio would last from 10 a.m. to 6 p.m. The evening before, the company manager or stage manager emails confirmation of the call times, so that people aren't sitting around unnecessarily. The first day of rehearsals is an exciting and nerve-racking time. They often start with a 'meet and greet' – weirdly, a part that many people hate. There's something about standing in a big circle and introducing yourself to your colleagues for the first time that makes people uncomfortable. In fact, starting work on a new show is a bit like entering the *Big Brother* House. The company comes together and for however long your contract lasts, you become extremely close and experience an incredible amount together as a team. On that first day, though, many people are strangers to one another. It feels very new and very raw. Hopefully within a day or two everyone is comfortable and starts to bond, which makes for happy families – but also better onstage chemistry and trust.

The plan, with most creative teams it would seem, is to get the show completed and learned as soon as possible, which then allows more time later on to make changes, tweak elements, tighten everything up – and rehearse and rehearse, over and over, until it's perfected. To speed up the rehearsal process, and get everything blocked and learned, there are usually several rooms being used at the same time, and the schedule will always be devised to make the most efficient use of time and space.

The musical director will almost always begin the rehearsal period by teaching or 'note-bashing' the songs to the full cast. It's a good idea to record your songs, and especially your harmony lines, so that you can go over, learn and practise them at home; these days most smartphones can record audio. If everyone is on top of the songs, then it will be easier when the choreography is introduced.

Whilst the musical director is rehearsing the songs, the director may be in a separate room working on some of the scenes with the leading actors, whilst the choreographer will have another group of people (generally in the main room) learning some dance steps or rehearsing a number. There will always be one main room – the biggest – with the stage marked out in tape on the floor, showing where the wings and back of the stage will be, where certain set pieces will be positioned, and where the track lines will bring the set on and off. There are also numbers running equidistant across the front of the stage: 'o' is dead centre working outwards on either side, like this:

8 7 6 5 4 3 2 1 0 1 2 3 4 5 6 7 8

These numbers will then also be exactly the same across the front of the stage at the theatre, and enable you to have a reference during dance routines and scenes. You can glance down with your eyes, and ensure you're hitting the same place each time. A choreographer will also refer to them, often saying something like 'Can I just see what it looks like if you step to the left? Great, so that's number three?… Okay, and take one step further upstage, so you're in line with the middle track.' Then you've got a number along the front to line up with, and a track to line up with in the other direction. Remember that spot!

Rehearsals are amazing – because that's when you really get to figure out who your character is, and create your fully rounded performance. Becoming part of a team, learning a new show together, and working out how you can best tell a wonderful story is exhilarating. Providing the director is a good leader of a company, the rehearsal period can be a very happy and exciting time.

What tips and techniques can be used to develop a character during rehearsals?

Always approach a role with an open mind. Start by doing as much homework and research as possible before rehearsals begin, but don't force yourself to have a concrete idea of every aspect of your performance. On your own, you can work out roughly what you think about the character, what they think about themselves, the journey they go on during the show – but it's when you work with a director, the creative team and your fellow performers that the great collaborative nature of rehearsals comes to the fore. Think about life: our feelings change during a single day, depending on how other people make us feel or the situations we end up in. Likewise, it's when you're in rehearsals, in character, on your feet, surrounded by other actors, and in the situation, that you can really explore your options before making decisions about your performance. Every character, every scene, every line of dialogue, every lyric, and every musical number is in the show for a reason. They tell a story, and they (should) move that story forward. Focus on that sense of storytelling – what you're telling the audience, how and why – and find within your character, every line of your dialogue, every song, the ways in which you can support and strengthen that.

Just like in life, where we never truly know everything about ourselves, you'll never know everything about your character. They become like a very familiar friend, but however long you might be in a show – even a year-long contract – you never stop learning about them and finding new perspectives. Stay in the moment, responding truthfully to the other actors in the scene, and you'll find new ways of delivering lines or gestures, and the emotions you feel will change over time. In order to develop and give a truthful, authentic performance, you should:

- Be present in the given set of circumstance at all times. If you walk into the living room of the house you've lived in for fifteen years, for instance, you'd be very comfortable and at ease; if you're meeting your partner's parents for the first time in a place you've never been, you'll be slightly more on edge.
- Understand your character's perspective, and really feel what it's like to be in their shoes. This will come through spending time with them (and *as* them!), in rehearsal and in performance.

The more you know about your character, and how they'll react in different circumstances, the more spontaneous and believable your characterisation will be, and the more prepared you'll be to handle anything unexpected that happens during a performance.

How much freedom are you given to change or add bits to your character? Or do you have to follow strict instructions?

During rehearsals, most directors will encourage you to explore your character fully, working in a collaborative and playful way to try different options. The closer you get to having an audience, the more knowledge you'll have about your character, and you can make more decisions about your performance. And once the show has been set, certainly from a technical perspective, you will have to honour and follow what was finalised. If you've been lit downstage-left during the first verse of your song, then clearly you can't wander across the stage; you have to stay downstage-left.

During a long run of a show, it can be difficult to keep things feeling spontaneous and fresh. The temptation is to try to find new things, night after night, which begins to move your performance in a direction too far away from what was originally agreed in rehearsals. A resident director or associate director – who watches the show regularly, keeping it in check, and maintaining the high standard – will warn against this. They provide an outside eye, and can come in and say something like 'I love what you're doing, and you can keep the energy and urgency there, but don't forget that she really cares for him too, and doesn't want to push him away…' Suddenly you're reminded of a little perspective you might have gradually moved away from.

How do I prepare before a performance?

There are many different ways in which you can prepare yourself before a performance and get into character. Some performers have a very specific ritual of what they have to do before a performance, which cannot be altered – and can be quite extreme! Other people can just walk on stage without even thinking about it and turn it on. It all depends on who you are as a person, your acting method and style, the way you've been trained, and what you have found works for you through your experience in the industry.

I like to get myself ready slowly; rushing is a big no-no for me and just makes me panic. Even if it's a one-off show or concert, I lay everything out neatly on my dressing table. I start by doing my make-up and once I'm happy with that, I'll have a hot drink – normally hot water with fresh ginger, lemon and honey, which soothes my throat and clears away the cobwebs. Then I'll do my warm-up, maybe run through a few songs (especially for a one-off gig when I need to know I can remember all the lyrics), and get into costume. If possible, I like to see my other half, Andrew, before the show starts. It puts me at ease that he is out there – supporting me – and helps put everything else into perspective. Then off I go!

Before every performance as Curly McLain in *Oklahoma!*, I had to arrive at the theatre an hour before everyone else to have my incredibly straight hair put into heated rollers to make it curly. The director wanted my hair that way and I refused to wear a wig because I thought I'd look like a cross between Barbra Streisand with her 1980's perm and Little Orphan Annie. I wanted to have my own hair. The curlers were actually called 'benders' and were pink and lilac heated rods that I had to have my hair wrapped around once I'd used a curling serum, then they would be twisted and bent into shape and needed to stay in for thirty to forty-five minutes. Whilst I was letting the benders do their work, I applied my show make-up – and there was lots of it! Because Curly's a cowboy, out in the sun all day, he'd be rather darker skinned and tanned than me, a Welsh actor touring the UK. So I had to wear a dark base colour and lots of dark bronzer.

Next, I would wear a hairnet to secure the benders, and an elasticated headband placed around my head to hold everything in place, whilst I joined the full company on stage for a physical and vocal warm-up. I used to look like one of the old ladies from *Last of the Summer Wine* doing a few ballet stretches in the downstage-right wing space every day. After the company warm-up I used to have all the hair stuff taken out, my new curls styled into place and sprayed with a whole lot of superglue-type hairspray so it would stay curly for the next three hours (which, for the record, very rarely happened). At the half-hour call (thirty minutes before the start of the show), I'd put on my costume, because it was good to wear it for a while. The boots were really heavy, the suede horse-riding chaps were restrictive, the gun and holster made it even more awkward to walk, and the cowboy hat (which squashed all my wonderful curls after all that effort) was the final touch to this happy-go-lucky cowboy's outfit.

When I looked in the mirror I really looked nothing like my usual self. I was a cowboy with curly hair, dark skin, scruffy clothing and clumpy boots, which made becoming a different person so much easier. On the beginners' call, I would head to the stage and, during the five-minute overture, I would think about where Curly has just been, where he's going and why he's going there, and focus solely on his intentions for the first scene. I always think of only one scene at a time, because if you focus too far ahead, you are anticipating the future and will not be truly present in the moment. You start giving an automatic, rather than a truthful or honest performance.

The wonderful thing about playing Elphaba in *Wicked* is that the physical transformation naturally takes you a lot of the way there. I'm quite a 'girly girl', I have very blonde hair and like pretty things – and a heel! Elphaba couldn't be further away from me, so the transformative journey into character began as soon as I walked into my dressing room, tied my hair up and started turning green. The green make-up was always done by one of our fantastic make-up team, usually taking around twenty minutes to apply. I would then go down to the company warm-up on stage and prepare my body and voice for the mammoth task of playing the Wicked Witch of the West.

The moment it would all come together for me was returning to my dressing room after the warm-up and having my long black wig put on and then getting into costume. I would really feel like Elphaba when I finally put on my flat leather boots, made my way downstairs, grabbed my suitcase and stood at the back of the stage behind the sliding doors. What's interesting is that Elphaba is a very solitary person, and having spoken to many actresses who have played her, we all agree that her role is a pretty lonely one to play as well. During the show there is so much to do that you never really get to speak to anyone else offstage. From the moment the curtain went up it was pretty much just me and my dresser Troy working together – which was lovely, of course, but as far as chatting to anyone else in the cast throughout the show goes... not a chance!

Once I had settled into the run of *The Book of Mormon*, and had time to establish who Elder Kevin Price was for me, I found it a relatively quick and easy process to get into character. His intentions are obvious: he aims to be the best at everything he does, he wants to change the world – and everyone in it – through sharing the beliefs of the Mormon Church, and he has no doubt that he is destined for the maximum success possible during his two-year mission in Uganda. He doesn't have any insecurities, he is the golden boy and the ideal example of the perfect Mormon in every sense. In his head anyway.

After my physical and vocal warm-up, having my hair styled with the typical Mormon side-parting by our hair supervisor, and putting on my costume – I would jump around a bit with a huge smile on my face to get into that enthusiastic, energised, always-smiling demeanour. Elder Price's smile is particularly perfect. Then I'd head to the stage and stand in my preset position behind a huge scenery cloth. Whilst standing there I would think through all of Kevin's intentions, as mentioned above, and all the reasons he believes he's destined for greatness, which would put me in the right frame of mind for the moment the cloth flew out. I would be revealed, silhouetted and centre stage, ready for a strong and steady walk down to the front, and confidently ringing the (imaginary) doorbell, and setting off on the journey of the show.

How do I keep my performance fresh when I'm singing the same songs every night, eight times a week?

It can sometimes become difficult to keep your performance fresh – whether your run is long or short, you've probably been rehearsing it for some time. If you invest properly and fully in the journey of your character, a song should just be a continuation of the storytelling, so you need to sing the words as if you were saying them for the first time. It's the most effective way of keeping the material, and your performance, focused and energised.

It is, however, easy to get complacent and then distracted during long-running shows – and this is when it becomes easy to forget lines, lyrics or make mistakes. You'd be surprised how much the body can perform on autopilot. We try to avoid that at all times because, obviously, it won't produce the most invested performance for the paying audience who may be seeing the show for the one and only time. Autopilot performing also means you're disconnected from the material and it can make a long show seem even longer – but sometimes it's a fact that the body just won't physically do what you want. Concentration becomes really difficult and you become easily distracted. Here's an example of what your mind might be doing during a song:

'On my own,
Pretending he's beside me.
All alone,
I walk with him till…

(What's that red light in the second row?
I bet it's someone's phone.

Oh my God, it is a phone.
Didn't they hear the bloody announcement at the top of the show? 'Please ensure all mobile phones are turned off –
Oh, but you're the exception, madam, you go ahead and keep yours on, and when the cast are trying to sing, you shine your bright-red light from your seat to let them know you are recording their performance.'
I bet that bloody thing is gonna end up on YouTube and will then be made into a compilation video of all the Eponines belting the big 'I've only been pretending' line.
I now can't stand that person on the second row for distracting me… Right, where am I in this song?… Oh yeah…)

But only
On my ooooooown.'

Applause.

The trick is only to pay attention to what you're saying and singing. Keep eye contact with anyone on stage you're interacting with. Keep in the moment. Focus solely on who you are (the character, not yourself), where you are (in the scene) and what you're thinking, doing, moving and saying – and *not* on the fact that you still have the whole of Act Two to get through before heading home for your Lemsip and an episode of *Downton Abbey*.

What should I do when things go wrong during a performance?

Unfortunately, there is not much advice to give for when things go wrong on stage. It will usually involve involuntary freezing and forgetting the English language or any sense of normal human behaviour at all. Both of us have made numerous mistakes on stage: we've made up lines of the script when we blanked, made random sounds that are more like animal cries, completely fallen over on stage and struggled to get back up, which reminds us of a time we worked together in *Wicked*...

I was Fiyero, opposite Louise as Glinda, in the opening scene of Act Two, where pretty much the entire company are on stage as the citizens of Oz, looking to Glinda the Good for reassurances about their safety against Elphaba. Fiyero gets frustrated because none of what is being said about Elphaba is true, so he storms off the podium centre stage, and heads downstage-right for a quiet, emotional scene with Glinda.

So there we are, me and Louise, acting the scene (beautifully, even if we do say so ourselves!), and then I turned to do Fiyero's dramatic exit, which involved running up some narrow stairs and continuing offstage. Off I went, missed my footing, tripped on a step, and landed in the full splits on the staircase. I struggled to stand up, pulling off bits of the leaves and branches from the scenery to help me, and when I finally managed to get to my feet, I just dropped my head down in shame and continued to run offstage. Two-thirds of the audience were laughing out loud, and the entire company were trying not to lose it altogether.

I was left at the bottom of the staircase, looking up at where it had happened, desperately trying not to burst into laughter. Then I had to look at the company, who were all grinning at me like lunatics, and finish a very emotional part of the scene. When I got offstage, Mark and I fell about, laughing until our stomachs hurt, and almost missing our next entrance. It remains one of the highlights of my career.

The thing is, mistakes happen and that's the joy of live theatre. It's not like performing brain surgery where every single thing you do is a life-or-death situation. If you forget your lyrics or make a mistake, keep calm. It will somehow resolve itself, usually by trusting your instincts and getting yourself out of it – but at the end of the day, it's just a show. The audience are unlikely to notice, and if they do (like in the case of Mark's impromptu splits) then they love the fact they've seen something totally live, utterly unplanned and unique.

How can I deal with doing things on stage that I'm not comfortable with?

An actor can be required to do many things with which they may not feel comfortable: kissing, swearing, scenes of violence or nudity. The rehearsal period should allow you enough time to figure out how to deal with these scenes until you feel completely at ease with them, before performing in front of an audience.

During rehearsal is when you should express any concerns you may have, and we recommend talking privately with your director about these anxieties – preferably before you have to rehearse those scenes. This will allow them to work out the best way to approach those scenarios in order to make you feel comfortable. Most good directors, though, should anticipate any concerns, and will have considered how to deal with them, without you needing to bring it up.

You must trust and feel comfortable with the people you are working opposite in all your scenes, but especially if it involves a close physical relationship. If you have a romantic relationship with another character, then we'd advise spending time getting to know the performer. It's unlikely that any intimate scenes would be done very early in rehearsals, which should give you time to get to know your fellow performers a little better. There might be an opportunity to do this before rehearsals begin too, if you know who has been cast.

The main thing to remember is that once you're on that stage, it is not 'you' that the audience is thinking about; it's the character you are playing. Each and every moment is only part of the production because it's important to the storyline, and part of your character's journey. So whatever the situation, you can deal with it all, providing you're experiencing it through the life of your character. Take, for example, the kisses that the two of us shared playing Fiyero and Galinda in *Wicked*.

The first one happens when Fiyero and Galinda (before she becomes Glinda) are on the dance floor of the Oz Dust Ballroom, having a great time dancing together – then suddenly there's a simple yet passionate kiss between them, in front of the rest of the students. There is an element of excitement that it's their first kiss, but they also know that, due to their popularity at the university, everyone will be watching them – which makes it feel a little risqué and rebellious. So that's all that we would focus on: how did it make us feel within the circumstances of the situation given at that time?

They share a second kiss in a very isolated place. Fiyero is playfully chasing Galinda across a bridge and she stops, leans in and lets him kiss her, softly and lovingly, and then it's interrupted by the rain. But in that instant, the two of us would really forget that the audience were watching us. It was all about focusing on the other person and allowing these characters to enjoy each other and that intimate moment.

The best way to deal with what you may consider to be uncomfortable moments is to immerse yourself in the character you are playing as much as possible. Forget the reality of the situation and being involved in it as yourself – which is actually what you should be doing at all moments when you are performing on stage.

How can I prevent my voice shaking on stage when I'm nervous?

Nerves are a totally natural response when you're doing something that makes you feel slightly vulnerable – even if you enjoy the activity (which is how we hope you feel about performing!). No matter how many times we have performed, whether it has been to thousands of people or just two, we still get nervous. It can be incredibly frustrating when you've finished a performance and you know you could have done so much better if your nerves hadn't got the better of you. So we know exactly what you mean when you describe your voice as shaking when you get nervous.

In fact, everybody feels nerves at times – and dozens of people asked a question about how to deal with them, so we know that it's very common. The truth is that some people just hide them better than others, so they never show any sign of nerves, and always seem confident. You have to learn to hide it too. Before you are about to perform on stage or in an audition, give yourself time to go and find a quiet space on your own; the toilets or bathrooms work well for this as the acoustics are great. Take some slow, steady breaths in and out, close your eyes, put your warm-up on your mobile, and gently do your exercises, focusing on your breathing – and then sing your song. Before you perform, take a few more slow breaths, focus on the character, and remember how easy it was to sing when you were in the loo! Be confident and in control.

When I first graduated from drama school, I used to get unbearably nervous before auditions. My voice would shake and my breath control would be so erratic that I couldn't sing as easily as when I rehearsed the song. My legs would also shake a little and I had to work really hard to look relaxed and confident. I still get nervous, but it has definitely become better over time – now it's more like butterflies in my tummy.

I think that nerves mean that you care about your job, and you want to do it well, so start thinking of them as being a positive thing, as long as they don't completely take over you and your performance. Harness your nerves as something that pushes you to do your best, and think of those butterflies as excitement rather than nerves. Always remember: you love performing, so why be nervous about it?

How does it feel to step out in front of an audience?

The first time you perform a new show or role in front of an audience, there is always a feeling of nervous excitement and adrenalin, along with understandable anxiety. Nothing you do on stage is yet fixed in your body's muscle memory, and therefore a lot more brain power and concentration is required. Comedy scenes that have become predictable and unfunny in rehearsal are finally in front of an audience, so you can see how the reaction to them will change the pace and timing of the scene. All in all, it's an overwhelming feeling of euphoria. It's why we do it, after all: to have that experience performing live on stage and being in contact with an audience.

My favourite part of opening in a new show is hearing the overture play for the first time. The sound of the orchestra fills you with the adrenalin you need to be able to focus and take your performance to the next level. Hearing the climax of the *Ghost* overture on my first night in that show was such a buzz. It's such a well-orchestrated piece of music and makes you tingle just listening to it, but to be standing backstage in the dark, whilst waiting to make your first entrance, is amazing. I very often think of that first night.

How can I make a connection with the audience when performing, so that they feel like they have been told the story personally and were connected with the characters?

It's best not to worry too much about what members of the audience are thinking. This might sound quite surprising, and of course it's true that ultimately we're *only* performing for an audience. But we believe that our job as actors is to be as authentic as possible, and that we serve the audience best when we concentrate on telling the story accurately and honestly. The focus should be the other characters, the plot, and the journey across the entire show – then you're giving the audience everything they need to connect to the characters, and invest in the storytelling.

We've all been to the theatre or the cinema with a friend, and walking out afterwards your friend is saying 'That was amazing', whilst you thought it was really boring. The beauty of the human race is how wonderfully individual we all are, and how our responses to the same thing can be totally different. With this in mind, it's best to think to yourself: 'My job on stage is not to make the audience enjoy it; it's to tell them the story in the best way I possibly can.' And the rest is up to them! You're not forcing people into thinking or feeling something (which you can't do anyway), and it takes away the pressure of having to be 'good' every night. Realistically, you can't be 100% 'good' every night anyway – but you can be 100% *honest*.

What are your thoughts on bootlegging, recording or filming during a performance?

We both feel strongly about this. First of all, there is an announcement at the beginning of every show – or in the programme at the very least – that unambiguously states that 'The use of photographic or recording equipment is STRICTLY prohibited.' Why people then go ahead and ignore this we don't know. Why not sit and enjoy a performance rather than focus on trying to record it? The recordings are never good quality, the sound is always terrible, and the visual is usually foggy or wobbling between the stage and the back of someone's head.

It's also incredibly distracting to be on stage looking out into a dark auditorium but being able to see a bright-red light blinking at us or a phone screen lighting up someone's face. We really can see it – and it does have an effect on performers. It completely takes us out of character and makes us feel annoyed that someone is recording us without permission.

If you were on a train and somebody fixed a camera on you and started recording, how would you feel? Vulnerable? Self-conscious? Angry? That's how we feel too! This footage usually ends up on YouTube where people comment on it. How can someone comment on something without being there and experiencing the entire show and the atmosphere of the live performance? Taken out of context, these videos are never great. As actors we also have bad days when maybe a note doesn't come out as well as we'd hoped, or we have issues with being able to hear the orchestra properly, or a million other things that can happen in live theatre. This video is then broadcast to the world and is out there for all to criticise.

There is a brilliant video on YouTube called 'Patti Lupone stops *Gypsy* mid-show to yell at a photographer'. It makes wonderful viewing (well, listening actually, since it's just an audio recording – but the captions are worth reading too), because the great American actress, Patti Lupone, literally stops the show to berate someone taking illegal photographs of her. She expresses exactly the feelings of anger and disrespect that performers feel when we see people ignoring the request not to record, film or photograph our performances. (The only ironic thing about it is that someone other than the photographer she's yelling at has clearly recorded the whole thing and uploaded it onto YouTube!)

We do appreciate that YouTube and social networks are a great and essential way to promote theatre and to showcase talent, and we also understand that the majority of people who put videos and recordings out there are doing it because they genuinely love a performance or a performer, but why not wait for the opportunities like concerts or cabarets, when the performer accepts it will probably be recorded, or just wait for the professional footage, which will be far more enjoyable to watch for everyone? Don't waste your ticket money by gripping a mobile phone to your chest wondering if you're going to get caught. Sit back and enjoy the experience and get the most out of your trip to the theatre.

What is it like taking over a role from somebody else?

When you get cast in an existing show, and you're taking over the role from somebody else, there are some wonderful opportunities. To a certain extent, you have to learn what was being done before, so that your performance will work within the existing show – on an emotional level, in the relationships with other characters, and with your physical movements around the stage. So there's an element of being told: 'Press that doorbell in that way', 'Step out of the bubble on that lighting change', or 'Raise the broomstick on that note.' You're also mindful that you're joining a very close-knit family of performers on the show, who have to get used to another person's performance, and the similarities and differences you might bring to the company.

But you can't just offer an exact replica of another actor's performance. It wouldn't be authentic. You have to find and develop your own performance. Remember that you've been cast for a reason – and that the creative team believe that you can do it. You can deliver your lines with the same intonation, sing the same notes in the same order, stand the same way, make the same gestures and movements, but it's still *you* within the character and giving that performance. Keep the focus on your own performance, and its authenticity, rather than trying to give a carbon-copy portrayal.

What is it like being an understudy? Do they literally wait in the wings in costume?

Understudies are *not* standing, in full costume, in the wings, waiting for the lead performer to have an accident or lose their voice, so that they can triumphantly save the day! In most cases, understudies are members of the ensemble, so they'll already be performing their own track (their own scenes and songs, their positions on stage, their vocal lines and so on, over the course of a performance).

Understudying is hard work, as you have to learn up to three or four other roles, on top of your demanding role in the ensemble. Extra rehearsals are called for understudies to practise and prepare, and most productions will have understudy runs periodically, in which all the understudies perform their leading roles, sometimes to an audience of friends and industry insiders. You have to keep a lot in your head, you'll never get as much time to rehearse as the original performer, you have to be prepared to go on at a moment's notice – and all the time you know that an audience may let out a collective sigh of disappointment if they hear a star performer is off and you'll be taking their place. Having said that, understudies can be extremely talented, and it's very common that they are cheered to the rafters at the end of performances, when the audience realise that they were just as good (or maybe even better!) than the performer they were covering.

If, for whatever reason, the understudy has to take over *during* a performance, then they would be taken out of the ensemble, put into correct costume, make-up, wig, be mic'd up, and take over at the earliest possible moment in the show (usually without stopping the performance). And a swing would then take the understudy's role in the ensemble.

Being a swing is just as hard work as being an understudy, if not even more so! These are the talented people whose job is to know *all* of the parts in the ensemble and be able to do any track at any time. A swing can be required to learn anything from two to twenty tracks, and be expected to know them off by heart at the drop of a hat. On many occasions if there are lots of people off sick or on holiday, the swing will have to cover two or three parts from each of the tracks, performing the parts that are integral to the show; for example, scripted lines from different featured peasants in *Les Mis* or a pas de deux dance combination in the Havana section of *Guys and Dolls*. It's a tough job that sadly doesn't receive the credit it deserves. You have to have a very intelligent, logical mindset – and it helps to have a lot of common sense too.

It is becoming more and more common that some big shows will employ standby performers. These actors are employed to be in the theatre at all times, solely to understudy a lead role, or small number of leading roles, without being in the ensemble as well. *Wicked*, for instance, has a standby Elphaba, and another performer as a standby Galinda. *Spamalot* in the West End had one actor who was standby for King Arthur, Sir Galahad and Sir Lancelot. A standby can be quite well paid, considering they are often just sitting backstage waiting in case they are required – though they do have to be very talented and able to give the performance required of a leading role.

What do actors do between matinee and evening performances on the same day?

EAT EAT EAT!! I always have to eat a high-energy meal in order to get through the next show. Some actors have a little nap, but for me that means I have to start my vocal warm-up all over again as my voice drops down to my boots whenever I sleep. During my time in *Ghost*, I often went to the gym in between shows to keep the energy going, and then I'd sit in the steam room, which was good for my voice. When I've been on tour in different places I'd try and go to a good local restaurant or café recommended by one of the theatre staff. Most of the time, though, it's a social time where you hang out with some people in the cast or meet up with a friend who is nearby. The most important thing is that you are back in the theatre before the evening performance, in time for the half-hour call.

What to do during those precious few hours between the matinee and evening performances completely depends on the actor and the role they are playing. For example, when I was playing Eva Peron in *Evita* and Elphaba in *Wicked*, both hugely demanding roles vocally, I found that I needed to stay in my dressing room between shows, eat straight away so there was time for my meal to digest, and then keep quiet, relaxing my voice and body.

I found that having a sleep didn't really help as, like Mark, my voice would drop so much that it would be an effort to get it going again for the evening show. Then there are other roles which aren't quite so much of a strain on my voice, where I'll go out to eat between shows, get some fresh air and keep my energy up. Everyone has different ways of relaxing, though, so do whatever you find works best for you.

How do I stay healthy in order to perform eight shows a week?

Having played Elphaba in *Wicked* and Elder Price in *The Book of Mormon* – two of the largest and most demanding roles in contemporary musical theatre – we think we're particularly well qualified to answer this one! So here are our top tips for making sure you can perform at your best for eight performances a week:

- Sleep – Aim for at least eight hours of sleep a night. The body is only completely resting when it is in a deep sleep, which allows us to go into our neutral state and recover from any fatigue as much as possible.
- Vocal preservation – When performing roles that have a heavy vocal demand the reality is that, most of the time outside of the theatre, it's best not to speak. This can be difficult, frustrating and sometimes very lonely because it involves spending a lot of time by yourself. We both also go for what is called 'vocal massage' where a trained therapist will massage the muscles surrounding your voice box and help to relieve tension. It feels

quite odd but the release is wonderful and your voice feels much more open afterwards.

- Water – Drink at least three litres of water every day. Water is like medicine for singers; if you don't drink enough, the voice becomes more tired and it increases your chances of getting sick. Steam inhaling is a fantastic way to keep well hydrated, clear your passageways and relax your throat. You can purchase steam inhalers in chemists or online – or do it the old-fashioned way: put hot water into a bowl then slowly and carefully breathe the steam in through your nose and out through your mouth. Putting a towel over your head helps to keep the steam focused on the right areas and last longer.

- Food – Follow a healthy and balanced diet. This is very important and is also extremely difficult to coordinate around an eight-show-week schedule. There is a difference between eating healthily and eating what is good for you physically and vocally within the demands of being on stage. We aim for a healthy balanced diet – especially the right amounts of protein, iron, carbohydrates and good fats. If you don't fuel your body correctly, when you try to give the performance expected of you, you will run on adrenalin only. Then, when the adrenal glands become fatigued, the job gets really tough because the body starts to shut down.

  There are certain foods that are not recommended for singers: dairy products create a mucus which not only clogs the throat and makes you sound phlegmy, but can slow down the digestive process and create acid reflux, which sometimes affects the voice and gives you a sore throat. Foods that are high in their acidic content – i.e.

tomatoes, citrus fruits, spicy foods, etc. – can have the same effect. Caffeine can dry you out.

It is important to allow at least a couple of hours after eating before lying down, because if the food isn't digested properly, that can also create acid reflux. This can be difficult because after a show you can get really hungry as you've just worked extremely hard. The way we deal with this is just to graze on small snacks throughout the show; a handful of nuts, a protein bar or some chicken. Eating properly is the hardest part of maintaining your health to perform eight shows in a week. It is wise to speak to a nutritionist who understands the demands of theatre schedules for advice if you are unsure of exactly what you can eat.

- Exercise – It's important to do physical exercise other than the show itself to release the endorphins which make you feel good and also to keep you fit.
- Rest – In a different way to sleeping, it's vital to listen to your body and allow it to sit or lie down and rest when it needs to. We wake up some mornings and feel there's no way we will get through the show that night, but by resting and staying quiet it's surprising how the body can recover and be ready to get into show-mode when it's required.

- Warming up – It is vital to warm up vocally and physically for every show. Listen to the needs of your body and voice and allow it the appropriate time to get into show-mode without forcing it to do things it's not ready to do. In the same way you would stretch your body out after exercise, your voice needs to be brought back to a relaxed state after having had pressure put on it through singing, so warm your voice down with some gentle humming.
- Distraction – The pressure of performing can be intense, so it's important to lead a healthy social life and, whenever possible, to enjoy being away from work. Aim to have hobbies or interests that are nothing to do with the show. As actors, our jobs consume the majority of our lives and so it's vital not to let work devour your life completely.

When you work in a musical in the West End, it is an Equity rule that all actors must attend a full-company warm-up, which generally speaking involves a ten-minute physical and ten-minute vocal warm-up. This rule doesn't exist in America, where actors can just turn up for the half-hour call and the responsibility lies with them to ensure they are ready to perform by the time the show goes up.

When I first started *The Book of Mormon* on tour of North America I was anxious that I wouldn't have the opportunity to warm up in the way I needed to. However, I learnt to prefer it that way, because it allowed me time alone in my dressing room to figure out what my body and voice needed to get me in the right state to perform the show. Sometimes my voice warms up in ten minutes, other times it takes a very gradual and gentle forty-five, but now I like having the time to control that myself. The only downside is not having the chance to see the full company as a group, communicating and connecting with them, before the show begins.

It was such a big deal for me to head over to North America to perform in the touring production of *The Book of Mormon* – not just getting the role (though that was a big deal, of course), but the fact of living and working on the other side of the world, away from my entire support system: my family, friends, flatmate, agent, manager, doctor, osteopath, accountant, postman, window cleaner, bin man and the cat next door… It really did seem like I was kissing goodbye to so many things in my life, which was heightened because I was going to be in a touring show. A tour of that scale is like living in a bubble, and I'd be performing one of the most demanding roles in musical theatre, surrounded by a group of strangers I'd never met, for seven months. Little did I know that I'd end up being in the show for eighteen months, having an amazing time and visiting some incredible places.

I spent four weeks in San Francisco, rehearsing two or three afternoons a week, in advance of joining the existing company for the final five shows in that glorious city. The rest of the time I spent feeling anxious about whether I'd be able to survive the gruelling task ahead of me. I had many panic attacks and suffered really badly with anxiety and loneliness, to the point where I made myself sick with worry and developed a viral infection which left me in bed for seven days, completely helpless and feeling sorry for myself. I was in such a low place late one night that I called my agent, saying that if I didn't feel better in a few days' time I wanted him to get me out of the job and have me sent home. It was that extreme! Of course he calmed me down and helped me to deal with the pressure, as he's such an incredible agent and friend.

Our first performance was three days after Christmas Day 2012. We had our final rehearsal earlier that day with Trey Parker, one of the writers and directors of the show (and of course co-creator of the hugely successful animated TV show, *South Park*), and that night was my American debut, as Elder Price. The first Broadway show I ever saw was *Next to Normal* at the Booth Theatre, New York, in February 2010, and I remember promising myself that one day I'd be in a Playbill (the free theatre programmes given away at productions in the US). Now here I was, just two years later, leading a company of extremely talented performers. I felt so proud that all my anxiety disappeared and I was left with a healthy amount of nerves and excitement, ready to get on that stage and enjoy every second of a very special night.

Sometimes something exciting comes along at exactly the right moment. One afternoon, when I was feeling pretty low because my tour had been postponed for reasons beyond my control, my manager telephoned.

'Do you know the National Anthem?' she asked.

'Yes, of course. Why?!'

She explained that I had been invited to sing it before the Capitol One Cup Final – at Wembley Stadium, in front of 90,000 football fans, and millions more watching at home on TV! I thought she was joking at first, but she wasn't.

On match day, I had a short rehearsal in the afternoon and then had to go to my dressing room and wait to be collected and taken to the pitch. I don't remember feeling nervous as I was getting ready, just very excited, but when it was my time to go and sing, and I walked towards the pitch, I heard the immense wall of sound coming from the football supporters. I've never heard anything like it; it was almost primal and the sound literally went through me, my heart was racing!

What if I got the words wrong? What if I couldn't hear the backing track I was singing along to? What if I passed out?! I've never been so irrationally nervous. I was taken by the arm and led to the edge of the hallowed turf, I waited for a nod from the woman looking after me and off I went. The fans cheered, the music started and everyone sang along.

It was the most thrilling, terrifying, overwhelming experience of my life – and something I'd love to do again one day.

Part Four

SECRETS OF LIVING THE LIFE

Working and Not Working

What do actors do as their main job?

Believe it or not, acting *is* our main job! We understand why people assume that it's just something we do in our spare time – because that's what many young people do, growing up with singing, acting or dancing (or all three) as a hobby. But when you decide to become a professional performer you are trained to do the job – in the same way that anyone doing something specialist needs to be – and when you graduate you start looking for work and carving a career for yourself.

Having said that, it's not easy being a professional actor. There are often long periods of unemployment, and the pay is not that good even when you are in work. Many actors spend a lot of their time in other professions to earn money – teaching or tuition, waiting tables or bartending, corporate jobs, temping, and so on.

When I was in *Wicked* for the first time, in 2007, I was in the ensemble and earning about £550 per week. If you haven't started working yet, that might sound like a lot – but as soon as you take into account your agent's commission, your tax bill at the end of the year, travel, your rent, bills, food, classes, clothing and other random expenses, you're not left with much with which to enjoy yourself! And saving any money is practically impossible. I knew I wanted to buy property as soon as I could, so I applied for lots of teaching jobs – and for the duration of my entire contract in *Wicked*, I also worked as a teacher at musical-theatre schools such as Italia Conti, Millennium and Laine Theatre Arts, and also performed in workshops of other musicals whenever I wasn't required by my main job. Overall, I worked an additional twenty-six hours each week, so although I spent the year exhausted, I saved enough money to buy my first home.

What should I put on my CV?

Your CV (or résumé) is how most casting directors will first encounter you, so it needs to be clear, thorough – but not too thorough (long CVs don't get read; one page is best), and honest. You have to think of yourself as a product, and your CV and headshot are what are going to encourage casting directors and creative teams to 'buy' your services. Here are some top tips for your CV:

- Put your name and address very clearly at the top, and a small thumbnail of your headshot, in case the attached headshot gets lost.
- Don't outline all of your statistics, but ensure you include your height, eye colour and hair colour. You should get advice about your playing age range from someone who will tell you honestly. You might think you look 18 to 24, but maybe you're more likely to play 14- to 20-year-olds.
- Your training should always be prominently featured.
- Don't bother to list your academic qualifications (GCSEs, A levels, etc.) – it's not relevant – but mentioning a degree is fine.
- If you are a singer, your specific singing range should be included. Your dance expertise should also be mentioned (ballet, contemporary, street, tap, etc.).
- A list of the accents you can do is useful, but make clear (perhaps with an asterisk) which is your native accent.
- It's useful to include your specific skills, the combination of things that make you unique. But be honest (you don't want to get caught out saying you can do something that you can't), avoid obvious padding, and give relevant details. Here's an example of a good skills list:

  Skills: full, clean driving licence (including motorbike), advanced swimming (including snorkelling and deep-sea diving), jazz, tap and ballet (all advanced), puppet work, theatre devising and improvisation, horse-riding, roller-skating, stage combat (including medieval and modern weaponry), first aid (St John's Ambulance certified), fluent French.

- List your credits under different headings: 'Productions Whilst Training' or 'Non-professional Productions', and then 'Professional Experience'. Include the title of the production, the role you played, the venue or company, and the director. Don't be afraid to name-drop; if you've worked in a great production with a top director, the people reading your CV need to know about it.
- At the same time, don't be ashamed if you don't have many credits at first. Everyone starts from the same place of no experience. Some casting directors will get excited seeing performers without many credits, so they can feel like they're discovering a new talent and giving someone their big break. In time, you will take your non-professional and training credits off your CV, as you develop throughout your career and gain more and more professional experience.

What makes a good headshot?

Along with your CV, it's vital that you have a good, up-to-date headshot that realistically shows what you look like. You can't use one that is five years old, because – let's face it – you'll probably look a bit older. Your headshot is the first thing that the creative team and casting director will look at, so it's essential that it also looks professional and good quality. You'll need to pay a photographer to take the photos, and it can usually be quite expensive. The directory *Contacts* includes listings of photographers, but getting recommendations from fellow actors and friends is probably the most reliable way of finding a good one.

It's worth getting a few different headshots of you in different poses, and with different looks. Don't stray too far from a representation of your natural personality, so if you're fairly shy and softly spoken, don't dye your hair pink! Find a variety of looks that make you feel comfortable, and are generally quite neutral – so that a casting director can imagine you as Scaramouche, a rock chick in *We Will Rock You*, and also as Miss Honey, the mousey teacher in *Matilda*.

It takes time to figure who and what you are in this industry – which roles you're best for, and which you're most likely to get – and how to market yourself accordingly. You'll get lots of advice from people, which will sometimes be quite contradictory. Think about it on your own, how you want to portray yourself, and the performer and the person you want to be. Talk to your agent if you're thinking of radically changing your look – such as shaving off your hair or gaining or losing a lot of weight. Remember that certain alterations, like tattoos and plastic surgery, are more permanent than others!

How should I manage my money?

It sounds simplistic and self-evident, but you must be very disciplined with money. As an actor in the UK you're considered to be a self-employed individual, however much you're earning and whether you're in a show or not. This means that you won't get your tax deducted at source, when you receive your weekly or monthly wage like people with a regular income in a Pay As You Earn (PAYE) job. Instead, you need to file a self-assessment tax return by 31st January every year, and if you don't, then you may have to pay a hefty penalty fine. You need to work out exactly what you earned over the entire year, and then what you spent, specifically what tax-deductible purchases you made that were necessary for your career (e.g. a theatre trip to see a show you were auditioning for, your annual fee to appear in the Spotlight directory, gym membership, acting classes, make-up for a role, this book…!). To enable you to do this, you need to keep your payslips and your receipts throughout the year as proof of your income and expenditure – so don't throw anything away! Both of us would *strongly* recommend getting an accountant to manage your finances and your tax return. There's a price to pay, of course, but it will ensure the job is done in the way it needs to be, and it takes away much of the stress, pressure and extra effort.

One thing your accountant can't help you with, though, is actually paying your tax. The amount you get taxed depends on how much you earned during the *previous* tax year – which means if you have a great year of work one year and earn lots of money, your tax bill at the end of the *next* year will be very high. By that time, though, you might have had a period of unemployment and have much less money saved to pay it. It's why you should save whenever you possibly can, and consider your potential future tax bill as part of your monthly expenditure.

Paying tax is the one part of the job that everyone likes to pretend doesn't exist, and not enough people prepare and plan for it. All of us like to remember how we were as teenagers, relatively carefree, enjoying performing as a hobby, and not worrying about boring, adult stuff. Unfortunately, getting to grips with your finances is part of what comes from being a self-employed, professional performer. Tax is one of the least enjoyable facts of life.

Is any job a good job?

Everyone in this industry wants to be working – but a lot of the time actors, singers and dancers are expected to work for such little money, and sometimes no money at all. Sometimes it might be a fringe production, when everyone is there for the same reason, and no one is making any money. In those circumstances, working for free is a choice you can accept. However, there are times when producers are actually making a lot of profit from their productions – yet paying their employees barely enough money to live on. They get away with it, because there aren't enough jobs out there, and actors, especially young graduates, straight out of college, just want to perform, and be seen performing, as it might lead to other work in the future.

We are lucky to be able to do what we love and get paid for it, but we both believe that it really is important that you make sure you're paid the appropriate amount. Otherwise, producers will just continue to get richer, whilst performers will be considered as 'luvvies' with no self-respect who can be taken for a ride. For this reason, having a good agent to stand your ground and fight for your rights is essential. Ultimately, you love performing, but you also need to pay the bills. If you start working as an actor then the reality is that your hobby and your passion has become your profession and your means of survival. Part of that professionalism is ensuring you are properly paid.

From an artistic point of view, there are certain jobs that are not as fulfilling as others, but it's up to you to judge these opportunities on a case-by-case basis. Your needs and priorities will change throughout your career, and based on your experience. What we're prepared to do straight out of college will be different to when we've been performing for twenty years. You might want shorter contracts which will allow you more time and space to breathe; you might not want to tour so widely because you have a family; you might not want to dress up as a cartoon character any more. At the same time, not every job is going to be a major role in the West End transfer of a Tony Award-winning hit direct from Broadway. You have to decide what sort of work you *want*, and what you're happy and content to do – they may not necessarily be the same thing, and sometimes you might have to take a job because you need to be earning money. But if you really don't want to do something: don't do it. You need to be prepared to say no to something that doesn't feel right to you, won't inspire you, or you're going to be miserable doing.

I believe you can gain experience from every job, but I don't believe that 'Any job is a good job' in the same way that I don't believe 'All publicity is good publicity'! It's lovely to feel like you are in permanent work and filling every gap in the year, but if you are connected with a bad job it does stick with you a little bit. Always make sure that, before you sign the contract, you and your agent are happy with the deal and that it's a show you want to be involved in. If you have negative thoughts before you've even begun, it's not a great start. If the show isn't quite what you expected, the best thing you can do is ensure that you're doing everything to the very best of your ability. Don't get dragged down by any negative talk or thoughts on the show; just focus on the part you are playing and how you can make sure that you are remembered for that performance and not for the negative opinions surrounding any other area of the production. Remember that you agreed to the job and so you should keep your head down, remain professional, and always be a good company member. Once you have agreed to a contract, there is no point complaining about the job or what you are being paid – you could always have said no!

When I was about to graduate from college I was offered a job in the ensemble of *Saturday Night Fever* in Germany, understudying two of the lead roles. It was a great job offer, with a year's contract, and a fair amount of money. But I decided I simply didn't want to leave the UK at that point, so I turned it down. Many of my friends at college frowned upon my decision and made me feel very ungrateful, so when I was offered the UK tour of *Seven Brides for Seven Brothers* two weeks later, I didn't even allow myself the time to consider if I wanted to do it or not, I just accepted it straight away. It wasn't the best year of my life being on that tour, but I learned lots about the industry by doing it – one of the most valuable things being that I'd never let myself feel pressured into anything again or be influenced by other people's opinions about my life and my decisions. Every decision that's work-related in this industry will have an effect on your long-term career, life and happiness, so allow yourself the authority to choose wisely which opportunities you embrace and which you decline graciously.

Is success down to talent or luck?

I think you need a lot of both! Of course, you stand a much better chance of succeeding if you have talent, but you also need to have worked hard, always be at your physical and vocal best, and well-prepared. But there's a lot to be said for being in the right place at the right time. What good is buckets of talent if you sit on your backside and don't get out there and grab every opportunity?! I have been an understudy, I've been a swing covering lots of ensemble roles, I've played parts in small productions, and worked my way up to leading roles in huge productions – but along the way I have met people who have taken me under their wings and introduced me to composers, producers, artists, who have all in turn given me the most wonderful opportunities. For this, I count myself very lucky.

I don't really like the word 'luck'. I don't believe in it and never use it myself. Many people within the industry have casually said to me, 'We can't all be as lucky as you' – and, whilst I know they mean well, I somewhat take offence to it. Clearly they're not aware of how much I've sacrificed to achieve the things I have, and the tough decisions I've had to make to carve out the career I wanted for myself. I believe you need talent to get on in the industry, of course. But I think instead of luck, you need ambition, determination and focus.

Here's an example of what I mean. Back in 2011, during my run as Fiyero in *Wicked*, I had a night off and went to see *Ghost: The Musical*. I decided there and then that I would do everything in my power to play the lead role of Sam Wheat at some point in the future. Luck was not going to win me that job, so I called my agent immediately and asked him to talk to the *Ghost* casting director, expressing my interest in the show. I bought a guitar and learned to play 'Unchained Melody', as the role requires, I continued working hard at the gym, and I took voice lessons to sing through all the songs in the show. I turned down two other good job offers because I wanted to make sure I was still available if I got an audition for *Ghost*. This was all before the audition period had even started, and I didn't know if the casting director and creative team wanted to call me in for a meeting.

At first they weren't sure if the role of Sam was going to be available when the original cast's contracts were being renewed, but I asked my agent to invite the casting director out to dinner and suggest that they go and watch *Ghost* together and persuade him that, if the role became available, they *had* to consider me for it. I was eventually invited in for an audition, and after two more meetings I was given the job, replacing Richard Fleeshman, who was leaving the West End company to open the show on Broadway.

I had other jobs booked for the same time – four concerts, two Welsh TV shows, and my own one-man Christmas show in North Wales – so I regrettably had to withdraw from them in order to rehearse *Ghost* whilst still performing in *Wicked* at night. My point is that I didn't wait for luck (or the role in *Ghost*) to land in my lap, and it meant that I had to make difficult decisions and sacrifices. But if you want something badly enough, get out there and do what you can to make it happen. If it doesn't work out, for whatever reason, then at least you'll know that you tried your best and that it just wasn't meant to be. If you focus hard enough, you'll surprise yourself with how often you get what you wish for.

How can I maintain a social life when I'm in a show?

It's hard! But it's not impossible. The question you need to ask yourself is: what kind of social life do you want? Do you mean that you'd like to continue to party hard and stay up late with friends at the weekend? If so, that is going to be very difficult if you want to be at your best on stage for every show. Whether you are in the ensemble, a swing, an understudy or playing a lead role, you should take pride in the performance you deliver eight times a week.

You also have no idea who is in the audience on any given night. It should be enough that you want to give a great performance for the general public who have paid good money, but there could also be important casting directors, producers, directors, journalists and fellow actors in the audience, who will be able to tell if you've been up partying all night, aren't feeling great, and are having a bad show. We don't believe it's possible to maintain eight shows a week at your best standard if you are out most nights and not looking after yourself. It's hard enough to keep your stamina up and maintain good health, but it's even tougher when your body and mind are tired.

Having said all this, it *is* important to bond with your fellow cast members and enjoy yourself, so get the balance right and you can enjoy a healthy social life and still perform well. A social life outside of a show doesn't have to mean late nights out partying. You will usually have most of your daytimes free (apart from matinee days, obviously), so plan to meet friends and organise enjoyable things to do during the day, or on your day off (usually Sundays or – if you perform a Sunday show – on Mondays). If you are playing a role where you have to sing a lot, it's wise to think of things that won't involve you raising your voice too much. Many of your friends may work within the industry too, and have the same pressures and demands on their time and their physical health, so they'll be very understanding. You should certainly make time to be sociable and have fun, otherwise you'll end up resenting your job.

How can I balance musical theatre with other passions?

As the old saying goes, variety is the spice of life. Whatever you do, it is essential that you have a variety of interests and passions. If you have a career in theatre, or performing is a hobby (for now, at least), then it can very easily consume you. You can get to the point where you eat, sleep, drink and breathe your job. You need to be dedicated and disciplined; totally committed to your training, rehearsing or performing; be in great physical, vocal and emotional fitness; and able to withstand the knock-backs and the criticism, the highs and lows – so you need to have something else to focus on and enjoy from time to time. Too much of anything is not good for you, so if you enjoy reading or watching movies, a few hours of escapism, letting your mind wander elsewhere, will do you so much good.

It's not just for your own health that it's important to have other outlets for your creativity and your mind, but it's also good business sense to have other options. This industry is tough and so, whilst you will hopefully have long periods in work, we can pretty much guarantee that you'll also have times when you will struggle to find your next job. If, like us, you don't want to have to go and work anywhere else to earn money, then you should prepare in advance for those days of unemployment. You'll need to have other ways to make a living – so consider what else you would enjoy doing, what would fulfil you, and what you have a genuine interest in. Maybe go and take a short course in another field entirely so that you always have options. There is more to life than work – and as much as we enjoy our jobs, there is more to life than the stage.

Other performers have, from time to time, laughed at me when I've told them about a new project I'm working on alongside the production I'm in. They think I have enough on my plate with eight performances a week. But even if I have a long contract in a musical, I always need to be working on something else during the day: recording, exercise, learning a language, starting my own business –

or writing a book! I simply have to have something else to focus on or I'd go crazy. I adore my work but it's all about balance, and so it's equally important to me to spend time with friends and family, and to challenge myself by working on new things regularly.

I'm a very driven person, so much so that I find the things I do in my spare time have become work-related even if they didn't start that way. I go to the cinema to see most films that are released, for instance. It used to be something I enjoyed doing to chill out, but now it feels like research because I actively want to do more screen acting. Whenever I read anything now, even if it's a newspaper, I find myself reading in an American accent to keep practising my dialect. I took horse-riding lessons when I was in Atlanta with *The Book of Mormon*, partly for pleasure, but mainly so I could add horse-riding to my CV. Although all of these things are geared towards research, and becoming better and more rounded at my job, it's also giving me the variety of life we all need. The only time I completely shut off from work is when I'm enjoying being with friends and family, which is as often as possible and probably my favourite thing to do.

What's it like being on tour?

During my twenties, I did lots of tours, exploring every corner of the UK, visiting fascinating cities, and having a wonderful time. Every week on tour my performance would feel fresh and invigorated, because I was always in a new theatre with different audiences. But touring is also very hard work. You're living out of a suitcase and never get the chance to settle or even unpack properly. The endless travelling, sometimes from one end of the country to the other, can be extremely draining, so you have to look after yourself very well. I'm such a homebody, and so I miss my home, my family and friends terribly whilst I'm away; getting home for one day a week never feels enough. So I tour much less often now, and when I do it's often for one-night gigs and concerts. How you adjust to a touring lifestyle will depend on what kind of person you are. I don't regret it for a second – and some of the biggest, most fulfilling roles I have played have been on tour, such as the Narrator in *Joseph*, Lucy in *Jekyll and Hyde*, Sarah Brown in *Guys and Dolls*, and Eva Peron in *Evita* – so I do recommend it to anyone who gets the opportunity.

I love how close a company gets on tour, when you're performing, travelling, socialising and often living together. You can make some really great, lifelong friends. The pay is usually similar to a West End

contract, but you also get a subsistence payment towards your accommodation (your 'digs') on tour, which might enable you to save some money. It's also great when a tour goes close to your hometown, and you can invite everyone to come and see you perform: your friends, family, former schoolteachers, neighbours, old babysitter, and everyone who ever said that you'd never make a living out of theatre.

I remember taking *Oklahoma!* to the Rhyl Pavilion Theatre, the closest professional theatre to my hometown, towards the end of a nine-month tour. On our first night I stepped out on stage singing the opening number of the show, 'Oh, What A Beautiful Mornin'', and the entire audience started clapping and cheering. It was an overwhelming feeling to be playing this iconic lead role on that stage in that theatre, where I had performed in my first-ever musical, aged twelve, as Pierre in Sandy Wilson's *The Boy Friend*. It was one of the highlights of that tour – and of my entire career – and one of those rare chances that none of us take the time to appreciate, to feel really proud of myself.

I had done three national tours of the UK before I was asked to tour North America on the first national tour of *The Book of Mormon*, and I assumed I was prepared for it – which was a little naive! It's very different touring the US. The theatres are generally *much* bigger; the smallest are about 1,500 seats, all the way up to 4,500 seats, and these big venues really do affect your performance in many ways. The hardest thing is getting used to different sound in every space you tour to. Some theatres have incredibly designed acoustic auditoriums, so the sound just rings out to every person in the audience, whilst also sounding good from on stage. But many times performers will struggle to hear anything that they're saying or singing, because the sound falls dead or flat as it gets thrown out into the cavernous space. It requires a lot of trust between you up on stage, along with your fellow performers, the sound engineer and the musical director, to ensure that the sound levels are correctly set; that you are giving an energised performance, which will reach to every part of the auditorium; but that you're not straining yourself and endangering your ability to perform an entire week's schedule. Having experience of playing in different theatres – and knowing what you sound like – will really help in situations like this.

What's it like working in America? Are there any differences between British and American audiences?

I could write a whole second book as an answer to this question! First of all, I love both London and New York, and I don't think one is any better than the other. I've moved to New York, though, mainly because there is more work available – but there's a lot more competition for the work. I love American people's attitude, which is very common in New York, of not feeling the need to apologise for their existence. Whilst British people have an apologetic politeness and reserve, as if they're saying 'I'm sorry to be alive', in New York, many people have the confidence and pride to think 'Here I am, I'm special, I'm worthy.' It really makes a difference to their approach to getting work, where that air of confidence is encouraged. There's so much work happening in America that you feel casting directors and creative teams are desperate for you to be good, so they can complete their cast. Having a performer who believes in themselves gives an audition panel more of a reason to invest in them and trust them to take on a job in their production.

There are so many performers in the US that no one ever becomes complacent, and they're always working to stay on top form. At time of writing, for instance, I take acting class every Tuesday evening for four hours, I have screen-acting class every Thursday morning for two-and-a-half hours, dialect coaching every Sunday for two hours, as well as regular singing lessons and dance classes. If I did that in London my friends and peers would probably think I was crazy and wasting my money. In New York, I'm just one of thousands of actors for whom this is a regular week, as we constantly strive to enhance our skills.

The same attitude of American confidence compared to British reserve is true of theatre audiences as well. Getting a standing ovation is a wonderful thing, wherever it is, but in the UK it only happens if the show is really special. In the US, if people are enjoying something, they're happy to let you know it. It feels like American audiences stand up at the end of every show, as if it's as much part of their responsibility as applauding the performers.

How can I get other work, such as concert appearances, recording albums, or on cruise ships?

Extra performing work is not often something that you audition for, but will come your way, via word of mouth, as you develop and move forward in your career, gaining experience and building your reputation. For concerts, producers (or maybe the composer) might have heard your work on the stage, like your voice, and will contact you or your agent to check your availability and interest. But you can also be proactive: investigate who produces concerts and tours, and then contact those producers yourself, sending your CV, headshot and some recordings of you singing.

Recording work is similar. If you are looking to gain experience of recording in a studio, you can start by singing on someone else's album. Recording your own demo is a good idea – maybe three or four songs, not a full album, and not to release commercially – but a calling card, that will show off what you can do. Keep the cost down by hiring a pianist as your accompaniment, and contact local recording studios to see how much it would be to hire the studio and a sound engineer for a few hours. If you know anyone who is nifty in the technical department, then you could consider a do-it-yourself recording, with backing tracks downloaded from the internet, a microphone and a computer. Simple but surprisingly good quality.

Working on a cruise ship can be a wonderful experience, and a great way to save up lots of money whilst travelling the world, often performing in a variety of different shows on board. Auditions for these are generally discovered the same way as auditions on dry land – through an agent, in *The Stage*, or on noticeboards at dance and rehearsal studios.

What is your daily routine?

My own daily routine is much more regimented when I am employed. In order to remain healthy and prepared for each performance I'll tend to rest during the day, especially my voice. Sometimes I use my steam inhaler to relax and hydrate my vocal cords, and I eat well at lunchtime to avoid being too full before a show, which always affects my singing and performance in general.

I arrive at the theatre about an hour before the company warm-up so I can relax, put some make-up on, and leisurely start preparing for the show. There is nothing worse than racing into work late, feeling flustered and throwing yourself onto the stage. Then it's showtime! It's true that the adrenalin after a performance is always running high, but if I have a demanding role in a show, it's always straight home for me, to watch some TV, make a decaffeinated hot drink, maybe steam my voice, and off to bed. It's pretty boring, but it's necessary and rewarding when you walk on to the stage the next day feeling good. When I'm between jobs I'm not so strict with myself, but around audition time or when a performance date is creeping up on me, I slip back into my 'work' routine.

When you're not working, what is your daily routine?

In the eight years that I lived in London, I'm fortunate that I was constantly working as an actor, apart from about four months between jobs where I was teaching. When I moved to New York I took a chunk of time off from auditioning and working, to get into taking classes and having a social life. During that time I decided to take a job in a tavern near where I lived. Some of my friends laughed at me – they knew I didn't need to be a waiter for the money, since I'd saved a considerable amount from touring for so long. The reason I did it was so that I could enjoy meeting different people. I'd realised that *all* the people I knew and socialised with worked in the same industry and it had become a little dull. Working in this great little pub, run by an Irish woman and with mostly Irish and Mexican staff, really allowed me to enjoy a different side to my life. I loved meeting all the different customers and it felt like a great relief not being 'Mark from that show'. I was simply an anonymous, random, chirpy Welsh dude working in an Irish bar in New York, taking home a pile of cash tips after charming the customers with my good old British accent. So when I'm not working, my daily routine involves doing all I can to create variety in my life in whatever way. I never want to fall into the trap of feeling like a hard-done-by actor who *should* be in a show. I just enjoy life, knowing that it won't be long until the next job comes along to inspire me.

How should I deal with negative responses?

We live in the age of YouTube, Twitter and Facebook, and it's easy and instantaneous for people to broadcast to the world their opinions about you, whatever age you are or whatever level you're working at. Sometimes the comments can be lovely, but sometimes they can be very cruel. It's easy for people to hide behind a computer and write things about someone that are hurtful, and that will affect the recipient's confidence and feelings if they look at them. So although it's difficult to fight the temptation, our biggest piece of advice is: don't look at them! What exactly are you looking for? If you are searching for praise and admiration then you might find it, but you have to accept that there will also be the opposite. Not everyone has the same taste – honestly it would be a very boring world if we did – and you will not be everybody's cup of tea. It doesn't just apply to all opinions online, but everything from comments in the playground to reviews in national newspapers.

We have both been in this industry for many years and are used to the odd negative comment, which we've learned to brush off. That doesn't mean we don't feel affected by negativity, but what we don't do is allow those comments to completely rule what happens next. There's no point in worrying about one person's opinion. If it's something you think you can use as constructive criticism, then do so. Maybe the comment has some element of truth which you can use to develop your performance.

Remember whose opinion matters to you. Do you care more about one anonymous online critic, or the creative team? If they're happy, then you should be too. Listen to the advice and opinions of friends and family – they can be harsh and honest critics, but it will always come from a place of love and support. And don't forget the most important people: your audience! If they are clapping frantically and you get a standing ovation, who do you think is right? The person who wrote how terrible you were or the audience who clearly had a great night out and enjoyed your performance?

It can sometimes be hard to remain optimistic in such a tough industry, but when negative comments get on top of you (if you allow them to, or if you even see them in the first place!), try writing down five great things about yourself. You are a good person who works hard, who is respectful and who deserves success, so don't allow yourself to get too disheartened. If you find this hard, then meet up with some good friends who should give you a little ego boost, tell you how fab you are, and you'll soon forget you were even taking notice of any other nonsense. If you can't take the rough with the smooth then this isn't the industry for you. There are constant ups and downs, positive and negative comments, and you have to keep on pushing through all of this if you wish to succeed.

How do I avoid comparing myself to others?

The truly wonderful thing about the industry is how all types of people are required and needed and *celebrated* as performers: different looks, ethnicities, ages, heights, sizes, personality types, hair colours… That being said, there will still be other performers out there who look similar to you, have similar dance abilities, or sing with a similar tone. It is very easy to start comparing yourself to them: why are they getting so many jobs? Why do they always succeed? Why are they always in work? Or, if you're younger, why do they always get the main parts in the school play? You might start to feel jealous – which is totally normal, but ultimately unhealthy. When you ask these questions, you've started to focus on other people rather than on *yourself*, and what *you* can do to achieve the same level of success. We are all unique and we all have something unique to offer. Remember that you are *you* – and no one else can be you or bring the special qualities than you possess to a role.

If you are constantly being compared – or comparing yourself – to other people, and you feel it's damaging your chances at auditions and on stage, then it may be time to take some action and do something to make you shine in your own right. Maybe you look like someone because you have a very similar appearance? Think about what you can do to improve your chances of being recognised as you and not a lookalike of someone else; it could be as simple as changing your hairstyle. Maybe extra dance classes or voice coaching will help you sharpen your skills, so that you stand out from others. Feeling bitter or showing resentment towards someone else will only make you feel worse in the long run. Even if you're losing out on roles that you think you could do, you need to be gracious, wish someone well, and focus all of your attention on taking steps to get yourself to the place you want to be.

When I was at college, I was one of about seventeen boys in my year. For the entire three-year course, I was determined to be top of the class and worked ridiculously hard. So did a very good friend of mine – and we were always being compared to one another. He is tall, with dark hair and a similar look, and we are both experienced triple-threat performers having sung, danced and acted from a young age. We were often cast as the same character in college productions – me performing the role one night, and him the next; we were always the two who would be picked for any performing jobs; if one of us had a solo in a show, the other one would be given a similar solo, and so on... Some of the students and staff made a big deal out of this, but I believe that both of us were grateful that we had each other as healthy competition. We never became rivals, we were always friends and appreciated having someone to gauge our abilities against and compare ourselves to in a healthy way. Neither of us has stopped working since we graduated. Comparison with other people needn't be a bad thing – let it spur you on to success.

How can I stay positive in an industry full of knock-backs? And what do I do when I have days when I want to give up?

First of all, let us start by reassuring you that you really are not alone. It's hard to stay endlessly positive when you're faced with the challenges and knock-backs that are facts of life for every performer. We have all gone through periods of doubt, and we are all insecure to a certain degree, so what you mustn't do is give yourself a hard time for having these perfectly understandable and very common feelings. Instead, you have to know how to deal with them.

Knock-backs and rejection are going to be part of your life as a performer. You won't get every role you audition for, and sometimes you will go through a period where you feel you won't ever get a job again! This may lead to low self-esteem, lack of confidence, loss of motivation… All completely natural, but don't let these feelings take over. You need to retain a strong will to succeed, keep working hard and pushing yourself towards achieving your goals. For some people, it takes longer to achieve success than others, so remind yourself of your strengths, and that you are deserving of success. Having a strong positive attitude is essential – just don't let your ego grow too large.

If you get to the stage that you're considering quitting, ask yourself why you want to give up. Is it because it's hard work? Is it because you're not getting the auditions you want? Is it because you can't handle your nerves? If you ask these questions, it's useful to answer them in a very practical way, with logical solutions which can change your frame of mind and make you feel better. So, if you find it hard work, then remember that no one ever achieved anything without hard labour, so knuckle down and enjoy the challenge. If you're not getting the auditions you want, talk to your agent; if it's not working out with them, maybe it's time to change representation… Ultimately, only you can fix things. You can't wait for things to happen for you, so be productive and proactive in your career.

You also need to be realistic about your level of ability. Think of what you want to achieve, what will get you there, and then ask yourself honestly: 'Do I have the talent?' Asking this question isn't about letting your insecurities and doubt take hold, but about assessing your ability, as an outsider would, and being honest with yourself. If, for whatever reason, you don't think you have what it takes, it doesn't necessarily mean that you should give up. Perhaps there's something else that inspires you just as much within the same industry; something else that will give you a happy and fulfilled life, instead of the anxieties and struggles of a life without the rewards you wished for.

Are there any myths about working in musical theatre that are generally believed, but completely untrue?

A surprising number of people think that musical theatre is an inferior form of theatre – and that the people performing it can't act unless they're doing it in a musical, and that it's not as 'good' or as 'worthy' as a 'proper' play or 'serious' acting. Well, we're here to say: it bloody well *is* real acting!

A real actor invests in whatever material they are working on, whether that's Shakespeare or Sondheim, Cy Coleman or Caryl Churchill. Acting is about telling stories, and the fact that musical-theatre actors have to tell those stories through the medium of acting, singing and dancing is definitely *not* something that makes it any less 'proper' or 'serious' than acting without these extra elements.

In fact, as we hope this book has explained, being a musical-theatre actor is actually a very difficult, complex challenge, requiring a lot of dedication and hard work to perfect all three aspects of the job, and become a true triple-threat performer. We strongly believe that performing in musical theatre is a talent that should be appreciated and celebrated more than it is!

What's the best advice you've ever been given?

I'd love to be able to tell you some incredible advice that came from some huge superstar I met years ago, but for me the best advice is a few words of wisdom from the two people I trust most in the world, my mum and dad. They have always said to me, as most parents probably say to their children: 'Just do your best.' We put so much pressure on ourselves and sometimes it's nice for someone you love just to remind you that you can only be the best you can be, and that no one should expect more from you.

It's also vital to trust your instincts, something I've learnt from many wonderful performers throughout my career. If it's an acting choice when you're rehearsing a role, commit to it fully and don't doubt it; if something feels right then it probably is. When it comes to auditions and accepting jobs, again, trust your instincts. If you are forcing yourself to do something because other people are telling you that you should, then you're probably not going to be happy and fulfilled. We all need to earn a living, but if you're only taking a role for the money, you will be sacrificing your creative integrity in the long run.

The best advice I received was not given in one sentence, but is something I gradually learned. By working with my agent Mark Ward since the start of my career, I have developed the confidence to be brave. Together we have faced many difficult decisions on what jobs to say yes or no to, what auditions to accept or decline, whether a deal is good enough, or whether we should turn it down and request more money at the risk of losing a great opportunity. Mark has complete trust in my instincts and my ambitious mentality, and I rely on the advice and support that he gives me. If you want to sustain a career in this industry, then being brave is essential.

What are the most rewarding aspects of your careers?

There are so many rewarding elements to having the careers we've always wanted and the jobs we love. We all have to work to live, but to have the opportunity to do something that satisfies us, professionally and personally, physically and emotionally, is wonderful. So that's the first reward: getting paid to do what we love! We have both worked hard and slowly inched our way up the ladder by starting in the ensemble, understudying, taking unpaid workshops in order to work with particular writers or directors, and finally getting lead roles in musicals in the West End and North America. There aren't many careers out there that offer such enormous variety, with every job being so different, unique and challenging. This career is often unstable and insecure, but the risk we take is rewarded by exciting new opportunities and a career that is far from dull.

To be a part of something that offers pure escapism for all different types of people is also a huge reward. Life can be tough in so many ways and for someone to be able to go to the theatre and lose themselves for a few hours, allowing themselves to be transported to another world, is so special and important. We entertain not just because we enjoy it, but because it moves people. We can make people laugh, cry and feel intense emotions just by telling a story on stage. It's an incredible feeling to see in someone's eyes that they have been affected by a performance and to hear them walking away talking about what a great night they have had.

Another reward we have experienced is how much a show or a performer can bring groups of people together. We hear many stories about how theatregoers have made friends with others who have the same love of musical theatre or are fans of the same performer. The friendships formed can be so strong, and the fact that they are made by a shared passion is remarkable.

It's a hard business at times, but the purpose of this book is to make you realise that your dreams are achievable. With hard work and determination, combined with your talent, you need to keep believing you can make it. And now we've told you some of the secrets, we hope to be seeing you on a stage someday soon…

Good luck!

If you would like to contact us, or ask questions for future editions of this book, please write to:

LouiseandMark@secretsofstagesuccess.com

A Postscript for Parents and Teachers

What's the best way to nurture young talent?

If you are the parent, guardian or teacher of a young person who wants to develop a career as a performer, you must first ask yourself: is it the young person who wants this career, or is it you who wants it for them? Do they actually enjoy performing? Or is someone else (maybe you!) pushing them to do it?

You should not and cannot live your dreams through someone else. And you must never make a young person do something that they don't want to do. Childhood should be a time of learning, development and enjoyment. Dance classes, acting lessons and singing tuition should be *hobbies* that the young person thoroughly enjoys and actively looks forward to doing. Dragging them to ballet class, because they show some talent in that field, all the while they're protesting that they don't like ballet, is counterproductive and cruel. As we've explained throughout this book, a life in the performing arts is hard work, hugely competitive and you have to be strong-willed and determined. You won't help foster a young person's love of performing and their ability to withstand a challenging profession by forcing or cajoling them into things they don't want to do. First and foremost, people (of all ages, actually) have to enjoy performing in order to do it well.

If the young person is talented and truly loves performing, then being supportive and encouraging is the first step. We appreciate this can be difficult for parents or teachers who have no knowledge or understanding of the performing arts – or how to kick-start a career in them. If that's the case, then seek guidance. Look online. Read this book from cover to cover! If your child shows potential and wants to start classes, then ask around at school to see where other parents or teachers would recommend, and see if any of your child's friends already go to one. There are likely to be local dance classes, maybe Saturday or summer schools, in your local area, as well as private speech and drama teachers, singing coaches and musical tuition. If you're considering a school, phone or email the principal, asking to be shown around and talked through the school's ethos. Ask questions about what opportunities are open to the students there: can they take exams? Are there opportunities to compete in festivals or do local performances? Can they recommend further theatre training and agencies? You want to choose a school that teaches well, but that is also a happy, creative environment where your child will be happy to attend. Always make sure that the balance is right between the child's performance training and their academic education. Even though we both knew that performing was all we ever wanted to do, we both worked hard at school and made certain that our grades were good enough to back us up if we ever wanted or needed to go down another career path.

Of course, not every young person who enjoys performing will want to do it as their profession. They may have other interests and skills that they are more passionate about, and may prefer to keep performing as a hobby, possibly one they will carry on doing in amateur theatre companies throughout their lives. Other young people will desperately and passionately want to make performing their career, but for whatever reason – bad luck, poor attitude, injury, lack of talent – never quite make it. But don't let a lack of adult support and guidance be the reason that they abandon their dreams. Nurturing young talent is all about allowing the child to develop in their own time, always encouraging but never pushing them. Give them the confidence, the opportunities, and don't clip their wings, if they want to pursue it. But never force them if they don't want to. Allow them to enjoy what they are doing at all times, and make sure that they are surrounded by support and love.

We thought that the very end of this book was a good moment to go right back to the very beginning, and describe how we were supported every inch of the way by our own parents…

I started dancing when I was three years old, performing for my family in the lounge – and charging ten pence a show! I enjoyed it so much that my parents took me to a small theatre school locally, where I started ballet and modern-dance classes. When I was old enough I started tap lessons as well, which soon became my favourite style of dance, and the one I was best at. I decided pretty early on that I didn't really enjoy ballet – it didn't come naturally to me, and I preferred dancing to a beat – and so I gave it up. There was no question from my parents about why. As far as they were concerned, I didn't like it any more and so they weren't going to force me to do it.

At about the age of twelve I took up acting and singing lessons, in addition to dance and, realising that I loved these as well, I decided that I would like to pursue a career in the performing arts. My dance teacher explained that if I wanted to audition for drama schools, they would want to see me audition in all aspects of musical theatre: acting, singing, and modern, tap and ballet dancing. And so I took up the ballet classes again. It still didn't come naturally, and I didn't really have the physical facility to do it brilliantly – but as far as musicality and style went, I gave it my best shot. All the way throughout my training – from the age of three, throughout school, classes and my training at Laine – the one thing that my parents would always do was check how I was progressing, and if I was *enjoying* what I was doing. They have never been pushy, just always incredibly supportive, and the pride in their faces when they see me perform makes me feel like it's all been worth it.

I'm the youngest child of four in a farming family from North Wales. I often wonder if, on the day I was born, my parents could have imagined what sort of person I would become, and what my career might be. I can guarantee that the last thing they'd have predicted would be what I'm doing now! My interest in acting, singing and dancing was not really considered normal, as a farmer's son in the area where we lived. However, my parents never made me feel anything but normal. There must have been times, especially for my dad, when he thought 'What on earth...?!' when I arrived home from dance class wearing sweatpants that looked like a shell-suit (or a bin liner), a T-shirt with a ballet dancer on it, and Capezio jazz boots (which support your ankles and have a Velcro strap with split-sole bottoms).

My parents knew nothing about any of the things I was interested in. And yet the way they handled that was amazing. They completely trusted me from a very young age to make all of my own decisions, and supported me in all of them. 'You want to play piano? We'll look into piano teachers...', 'You want to start ballet as well as all your other dancing? Okay, here's an extra ten pounds a week for private lessons, because you don't want to wear tights in front of anyone but your teacher!' They worked so hard to fund all of my extra-curricular interests, which was not easy given how alien those interests would have been to them. In a community that was pretty set in its ways, they didn't settle for anything. They may have found my hobbies more unconventional than those of my siblings and the other schoolkids, but they never once made me feel like I couldn't pursue what made me happy. Ultimately, you need to let your children make their own decisions.

Thanks

I'd like to say the hugest thank you to my parents, who allowed me to pursue my dream of being a performer. Without their support I'd never have had the training or the career I have had – love you, Mum and Dad. To all my teachers and mentors throughout the years, thank you for all you have taught me and still teach me every day. Thank you to my wonderful agent Michael Garrett and all at Global Artists, and our manager Rebecca Sichel-Coates, who encouraged me and Mark to write this book. To my Andrew, thank you for your patience and understanding and for accepting that I love to play 'professional dress-up' for a living! Lastly, to all my fans, whose constant love and support make it even more special to be in this industry – love to you all xx

I want to thank Dad and Mam for having a fourth child and accepting that he was wildly different to anything they ever expected. Thanks for supporting me every step of the way. Thank you to everyone who has taught me

something in my life and career so far – there are too many teachers, tutors, coaches, friends, family members, agents, directors, choreographers, singing teachers and colleagues to mention individually. I'm eternally grateful to everyone who has guided me in any way. Thank you.

Finally, we'd like to thank each and every one of you who submitted questions for our book. Without your intrigue and thirst for information we would have had to create a very different concept in writing it. Doing it this way felt collaborative and helped us to serve a purpose. Below are the names of everyone whose questions appear in the book. Sometimes, where multiple people asked a question on the same subject, it's been worded slightly differently, but we hope that you find the advice you need.

If the reason you bought this book is because you're an aspiring performer, we wish you all the luck in the world. Show business can be truly wonderful and we hope it brings you huge amounts of pleasure and success.

Adele Carr, Somerset; Aimee Whatson, Birmingham; Alice Howe, Essex; Alison Morris, Yate; Amanda, Orlando, USA; Anna Johnston, West Midlands; Anna T, Wiltshire; Anna-Maria Kollegger, Vienna, Austria; Aoife, Ireland; Ashleigh, Rhyl; Bekky, Cologne, Germany; Brendan Part, Dublin, Ireland; Brendan Turner, Indiana, USA; Cait, Newcastle upon Tyne; Caprice Lane, Shropshire; Carys Williams, South Wales; Catherine Coyle, Derry; Charlie Oliver D'Imperio, London; Charlotte Small, Cramlington; Chloe, West Midlands; Chris Birks, Rotherham; Courtney, Missouri, USA; Courtney Patton, Ohio, USA; Daniel Bastow, Sheffield; Danielle Alexander, North Yorkshire; Elizabeth Lieverse, The Netherlands; Ellie, South East; Emily Onsloe, Essex; Emily Stimpson, West Sussex; Emma Dallimore, Manchester; Emma Deacon, Hertfordshire; Emma Sweeney, Chelmsford; Faith Chamberlain, Sussex;

Francesca, London; Francesco Riccardo Dall'Aglio, Italy; Gemma-Marie, Canterbury; Geraldine, New Mexico, USA; Hannah Naylor, Bishop's Stortford; Harriet, Newbury; Harry Wright, London; Hazel, Long Eaton; Heather, London; Heather Kirk, Yorkshire; Holli Grice, Cambridgeshire; Holly Mann, London; Iain, London; India Edwards, London; Issah Nalzaro, King's Lynn; Jack Pilcher May, Leicester; Jack Robinson, Lichfield; Jack Scullion, Galway, Ireland; Jade Tyson, Leeds; James, Bristol; James Hinton, London; Jenni Walker, Southampton; Jessica Doolan, South Wales; Jo Gash, Wymondham; Johanne Hellman, Sweden; Jonny, London; JuJu Liao, Birmingham; Karen, Dublin, Ireland; Karl Piekaerts, Belgium; Katie Hook, Reading; Kayleigh Allan, Blackpool; Keira Guest, Salisbury; Kira Gorman, London; Kirsty Hogarth, Newcastle; Lauren Brushwood, Portsmouth; Lauren Novelli, Cheshire; Lauren Rees, Northamptonshire; Lauren Steele, Shropshire; Leanne, Padiham; Leigh Dobson, Bromley; Lexi Goodland, Northampton; Li-Lee, Essex; Lucas Cooper, Chatham; Luke Cooper, Rutland; Luke Martin, Devon; Lynn James, North Tyneside; Maggie S., Washington DC, USA; Martin, Northampton; Martin Battey, Ipswich; Matthew Neuenhaus, Birmingham; Matthew Parsons, Northamptonshire; Megan Lapper, UK; Melissa Harvey, Cornwall; Michelle, Washington DC, USA; Mikayla, Australia; Naomi Finlayson, Fife; Neil Kelso, Winchester; Nikki Hayes, Hartlepool; Olivia Moloney, Warwickshire; Oscar Gutierrez, Mexico; Phoebe Henderson-Pennington, Leicester; Rebecca, Manchester; Roger Crowther, Newcastle upon Tyne; Ross Bickerdike, The Lake District; Sam Mead, Newcastle; Sam Ryb, London; Sara Richards, England; Sarah Tanner, Southampton; Sarah Tolland, Glasgow; Sarah Yewman, Kent; Selena Zafar, Manchester; Shiri Fileman, Leeds; Sophie Benson, Guildford; Stacey Helmore, South London; Steph, Middlesbrough; Suvi Antila, Tampere, Finland; Tasha Hyde, Chippenham; Thea Peterson, San Antonio, USA; Tristan Josef, Los Angeles, USA; Vicki East, Kent; Wafi Habib, Brunei; Zachary Manlapid, San Diego, USA.

Index of Questions

Part One: Secrets of Learning Your Craft

Training and Developing

A Postscript for Parents and Teachers

www.secretsofstagesuccess.com

www.nickhernbooks.co.uk